# Hampton in the Bygone Days

## 400 YEARS ON THE VIRGINIA PENINSULA

Parke Rouse Jr.

Compiled and Edited by Wilford Kale

# VIRGINIA
## POPULATED PLACES

| | |
|---|---|
| 100,000 – 499,999 | ● Norfolk |
| 25,000 – 99,999 | ● Roanoke |
| 24,999 and less | · Monterey |
| State capital | ★ *Richmond* |
| Urban areas | |

The lowest elevation in Virginia is sea level (Atlantic Ocean).

WEST VIRGINIA

KENTUCKY

Clifton F
Covington

Salem
Roano
Bl
Bluefield
Blacksburg
Radford
Pulaski
Wytheville
Norton
Marion
Abingdon Mt Rogers
Bristol +5729 Hillsville Martinsville
Galax
Danv

TENNESSEE

NORTH CAROLINA

River
Clinch

# Hampton

## *in the Bygone Days*

## 400 YEARS
## ON THE VIRGINIA PENINSULA

Parke Rouse Jr.

Compiled and Edited by Wilford Kale

Design by Marshall Rouse McClure

AN OFFICIAL PUBLICATION OF
## Hampton's 400th Anniversary
## *1610–2010*

THE DIETZ PRESS
Petersburg, Virginia

*For Marshall Rouse McClure:*
*It was her idea and she nurtured it.*

THE DIETZ PRESS
*Petersburg, Virginia*

*ISBN: 0-87517-137-0*

*13-DIGIT ISBN: 978-0-87517-137-1*

*Library of Congress Control Number: 2009938610*

# CONTENTS

# ACKNOWLEDGMENTS

This book would not have been possible without the help and genuine support of Ernie Gates, vice president and editor, Newport News *Daily Press*. He granted permission to use a number of Sunday columns written for the newspaper by Parke Rouse between 1980 and 1996 as well as publication rights for numerous photographs from the newspaper's archives.

Special thanks also to Susan Connor, librarian at the *Daily Press*, for her much needed and much appreciated assistance in looking for photos and various newspaper stories. She was always willing to go the extra mile.

Michael Cobb, curator, Hampton History Museum, allowed access to the museum's outstanding photographic collection and spent much time assisting with the project. Bethany Austin, museum registrar, made sure the museum's important illustrations were accessible and scanned appropriately. Without them, the project would have been in jeopardy.

David Johnson, curator at the Casemate Museum at Fort Monroe, provided much time and effort in helping secure significant photos

*John R. Wilt Collection*

**African American watermen prepare for day's work in the 1910s**

related to the military installation and early Hampton. His help and assistance was invaluable.

A very special thank you goes to Erin McMahon Black, special event coordinator for Hampton's 400th Anniversary, for her enthusiastic response to the book plan and her encouragement and assistance along the way.

Gaynell Drummond, special collections librarian at the Hampton Public Library, provided some surprisingly wonderful photographs and assisted in many ways as did Elizabeth Wilson, Virginiana supervisor, and Cathy Davis, Hampton Library assistant.

Robert Hitchings, director, Sargeant Memorial Room, Norfolk Public Library and Gregg Grunow, senior librarian, Main Street Library, Newport News Public Library System also helped secure important photographs.

Thanks to Dr. William R. Harvey, president of Hampton University, for his special assistance and to Andreese Scott and Donzella Maupin, assistant to the archivist, at the Hampton University Archives, and Wendy Korwin of the Reference Department, Earl Gregg Swem Library, College of William and Mary, for their help with story- and photographic-related materials.

Sue Ann Bangel, president, Peninsula Jewish Historical Society, went out of her way to provide material related to the early Jewish community in Hampton. Her help and that of her colleagues at the historical society were greatly appreciated.

Special thanks to Greg Siegel for allowing use of his extensive materials on Hampton's first golf course, to Duane E. Mann of the Chesapeake Bay Floating Theatre for helping us gain invaluable materials on Captain James Adams's "showboat," and to Will Molineux, retired bureau chief and editor at the *Daily Press*, for providing great material on old Hampton newspapers.

Thanks also to Claudia Jew, director, photographic services, licensing and publications, at The Mariners' Museum, for allowing us the use of photographs from the museum's collection. Steven Daily, Curator of Research Collections, Milwaukee County Historical Society, Milwaukee, Wisconsin, expended extra effort to provide a photograph of Brigadier General William "Billy" Mitchell, and Dr. Paul A. Levengood, president and chief executive officer, Virginia Historical Society, provided important images of George Percy and Robert Barraud Taylor.

Michael Cobb, David Johnson, and Dorothy Rouse-Bottom read portions of the final draft. Their suggestions and observations were very important and appreciated.

Mary Ann Williamson, to put it simply, is a world-class copy editor. She cleaned up errors, made copy more readable, and made this publishing process much easier. Her efforts cannot be minimized.

Thanks to Wert Smith and The Dietz Press for their faith in the editor and designer and their willingness to publish another Rouse book.

Last but certainly not least, thanks, and much appreciation to Marshall Rouse McClure for the idea to do this book and for supporting it and donating scores of hours to make it a success. Her expert design talent and her tenacious attention to detail made this project much, much better. Her husband, Glen, was patient and, most importantly, understanding.

My wife, Kelly, put up with far too much, and her abiding love and assistance always kept me on an even keel. My sons, Walker and Carter, let me use "their" personal computer and allowed me much time that should have gone to them.

A postscript goes to Parke Rouse for his initial story ideas and his uncanny ability to tell a good story.

—Wilford Kale
*August 2009*

# INTRODUCTION

This book is intended to give some insight and depth to various elements of Hampton's four centuries of history. It is not a continuous historical narrative, but rather historical vignettes of various aspects of the history of Hampton and earlier Elizabeth City County.

Marshall Rouse McClure, the book's designer, believed her father, Parke Rouse Jr., local historian, newspaperman, editor, and state agency head, had written enough stories related to the city of Hampton to formulate a book, especially appropriate for the city's 400th anniversary celebration. She had earlier designed a collection of her father's writings relating to Virginia's earliest settlement, *Jamestown's Story: Act One of the American Dream*. She was encouraged to pursue the project by Dorothy Rouse-Bottom, her cousin and strong supporter of Hampton's history, and enlisted my help as compiler and editor, the same role Wilford Kale had undertaken on the Jamestown volume.

The task began with a search for stories on Hampton and its environs written by Rouse over a forty-year period. The Rouse Collection at the Earl Gregg Swem Library at the College of William and Mary included a number of stories. A careful scan of sixteen years of his weekly columns in the *Daily Press* revealed still other remarkable vignettes. After about six months, the collection of Hampton stories was then pared to approximately forty-five for this publication.

The next task was to edit the material. In some cases, the vignettes, often written twenty-five or more years ago, lacked some recently uncovered material, which we believed would enhance the stories. Thus, we decided to make additions where we deemed appropriate. In seven cases, significant stories related to Hampton were not among the Rouse material, but we felt it important that they be included.

For example, Fort Algernoune, the first site of English presence in the Hampton area, was constructed in 1609 just two years after the Jamestown settlement and the year before English settlers came to Kecoughtan, the old Indian village, just across the creek from the fort. This was a story that needed to be told in this compendium. Hopefully, these extra chapters, written in Parke Rouse's style, do not take away from the collection.

The final element was selection of illustrations appropriate for each chapter. Modern photographs were rarely used, because in essence, the vignettes, with the exception of the of the Hunter B. Andrews chapter, relate to activities, events, and people of Hampton prior to 1950. Old photographs, steel engravings, newspaper drawings, and vintage postcards were uncovered to help tell the story of Hampton in the bygone days.

# 1 Fort Algernoune

EW REALIZE THAT Old Point Comfort—that small piece of land jutting out into Hampton Roads—has housed military fortifications since almost the beginning of the colony of Virginia. Long a part of Elizabeth City County and now in the City of Hampton, it was a strategic point in the early seventeenth century for guarding the shipping channels leading to and from the Chesapeake Bay and James River.

The earliest fort, Algernoune or Algernon, was established in the fall of 1609 by men sent from Jamestown as lookouts to guard against intrusions by Spanish ships. This site was just thirty-two miles by water downriver from the Jamestown fort.

George Percy, new president of the colony's council and the eighth son of the eighth earl of Northumberland, sent Captain John Ratcliffe, one of Jamestown's leaders, to Point Comfort to establish the fort. Percy named the fort Algernoune after his brother, the ninth earl of Northumberland. Constructed of earthworks and boards "10 hands high," the fort was initially manned by between thirty and fifty men. It was built across the Hampton River from Kecoughtan, an Indian village somewhat friendly toward the Englishmen.

Not long afterward, Ratcliffe was killed during a skirmish with some Powhatan Indians while trading up the Pamunkey River. Captain

*Virginia Historical Society*

**George Percy**

James Davis, newly arrived with the pinnace *Virginia*, one of the colony's supply ships, took command at Algernoune, succeeding Ratcliffe.

Ironically, Captain Davis's work in Virginia connected both colonies established by the English in 1607—one at Jamestown settled in May and the other near the mouth of the Kennebec River in Maine, settled in August.

Davis had been one of the leaders of the Maine colony—often referred to as the Popham Colony after England's Lord Chief Justice Sir John Popham, the colony's chief benefactor.

The Maine colony lasted a little over a year with the settlers returning to England in 1608. During that brief sojourn the settlers constructed the first English vessel built in the New World and named it *Virginia*—the name originally given to the entire land area along the east coast from the Carolinas northward.

Little has survived describing the first vessel "of noteworthy size" built in North America, except that it was a thirty-ton pinnace. Recently some citizens of Maine have undertaken to build a reconstruction of that first ship, but few plans of small early seventeenth-century sailing vessels have been found. There was, however, a small sketch of the *Virginia* drawn on an early map of the Maine fortification.

That ship was probably less than fifty feet long with a beam of approximately fourteen

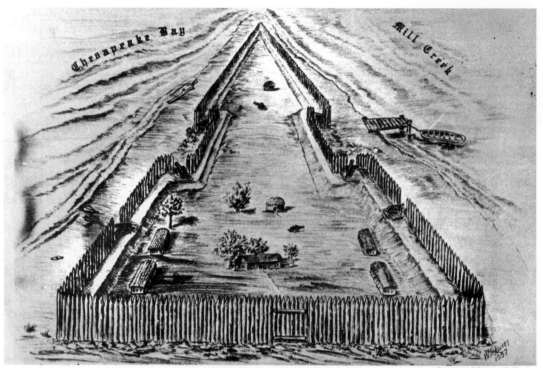

An artist's conception of Fort Algernoune circa 1610

feet, six inches. Experts believe it would have been rigged "as a modified barque with a square-rigged main mast, a much smaller second mast that was gaff rigged, and a small square sail under the bowsprit." By comparison, two of the three ships in the small fleet that brought 105 settlers to Jamestown in 1607 were the pinnaces—*Godspeed* and *Discovery*—weighing forty and twenty tons respectively.

William Strachey, a shareholder in the London Company who came to Jamestown in 1609, wrote an account of the Jamestown colony after returning to England. He described the *Virginia* as a "pretty pinnace." In those days, the word pretty meant sturdy, stout, or skillfully built.

The Maine ship—*Virginia*—with Davis in command, found its way to Jamestown in 1609 as part of the Third Supply Fleet. Sir Thomas Gates, designated the new governor of the Jamestown Colony, was in the supply fleet aboard the *Sea Venture* with Sir George Sommers, admiral of the Virginia Company. That ship was caught in a storm and beached on a reef at Bermuda. The other vessels of the fleet,

including the *Virginia*, proceeded to Jamestown.

The colony's winter of 1609–1610 was called the "Starving Time," when more than three-fourths of the Jamestown settlers perished. Such, however, was not the case at Fort Algernoune.

Percy, in his account of the colony, noted that "while all went to Ruine" at Jamestown, Fort Algernoune, under the leadership of James Davis, prospered so well that they fed leftover seafood to their hogs. Specifically, Percy wrote Algernoune "Beinge so well stored thatt the Crabb fishes where-with they had fede their hoggs would have bene a greate relefe unto us and saved many of our Lyves."

**Pinnace** *Virginia*

Seeing Fort Algernoune in such a prosperous state, Percy determined to move the Jamestown settlers down there, but as the plan proceeded, the survivors of the *Sea Venture*,

tain of the Henrico settlement in 1616. Some historians believed that Davis was among those settlers killed in the Indian attack of 1622, while others note that a "James Davis, Gent., late of Henrico in Virginia, deceased" is listed in Virginia Land Patents, Book 1. Captain James and his wife, Rachel, also were listed as "Ancient Planters" those people who arrived in Virginia between 1606 and 1616 and remained for a period of three years.

Across from Fort Algernoune, a settlement was formally established in 1610 at the Kecoughtan village seized by colonists under Gates. The Indians never returned, and the settlement grew and prospered and became known as Hampton, named for Henry Wriothesley, third earl of Southampton, who was among the leaders of the Virginia Company of London. The entire area became part of Elizabeth Cittie in 1619, Elizabeth River Shire in 1634, and Elizabeth City County in 1643.

—*Wilford Kale*

*Jamestown-Yorktown Foundation*

**Henry Wriothesley**

aboard two new ships, finally arrived at Jamestown in May 1610. Gates took over as Jamestown leader from George Percy and commanded James Davis to remain captain at Algernoune.

Later in May 1611, Davis was directed by the new governor, Thomas Dale, to reestablish the forts of Charles and Henry, built a year earlier on the Hampton River, and become captain of all three. In June 1611, a Spanish ship arrived just off Fort Algernoune, and Davis concocted a plan by which the shore party was ambushed and their leader taken hostage. The Spanish force then immediately left.

Fort Algernoune apparently burned sometime later in the summer of 1611, and Davis, according to Percy's account, "fearinge to receive some displeasure and to be removed from thence the same being the most plentifulleste place for food, he used such expedition in rebuilding of the same again that it was almost incredible."

History does not mention Fort Algernoune again. Davis, however, went on to become cap-

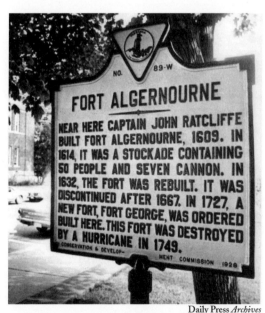

*Daily Press Archives*

**Historical marker at Fort Monroe**

# 2 Claiborne–First Entrepreneur

CLAIBORNE IS a Virginia family name you don't hear much anymore, but in early Virginia and Louisiana it was important. Retired Louisiana Representative Corinne Claiborne "Lindy" Boggs was a proud member of the Claiborne family, and her daughter, television news analyst and author Cokie Roberts, is another.

The Claibornes came to Virginia soon after Jamestown was settled, and in 1624 they patented land in what is now Hampton, the former Indian village of Kecoughtan. The first Claiborne was William, a 21-year-old emigrant and Cambridge University alumnus from Kent County in England, who started a trading system in Kecoughtan. He also erected a windmill and created a Hampton plantation where he lived off and on for the next twenty-five years.

The year he arrived in Virginia, William Claiborne was named by King James I to the eleven-member colony Council, to sit with Governor Sir Francis Wyatt and govern Virginia as a new crown colony. (Virginia had originally been a privately funded enterprise under the London Company.)

Claiborne served the crown enthusiasti-

*Appleton's Cyclopedia of American Biography*

cally as councilor and surveyor, traveling over Tidewater and dealing with settlers and Indians. He went up the James River by boat to Jamestown three or four times a year for Council meetings and was rewarded in 1626 with his promotion by Governor Wyatt to be secretary of state, the second-ranking job in Virginia.

In 1627, he was instructed by the Virginia Council "to go with a boat and sufficient company of men into the Chesapeake Bay and to discover any rivers or creeks ... and trade with the Indians for coon skins or any other commodity."

Claiborne's explorations of the bay led him to the present Maryland, then part of Virginia, where he named Kent Island for his native county in England. In 1629, the surveyor led a crown expedition against the Pamunkey Indians, who had been raiding English colonists along the York River, and forced them westward.

Claiborne's claims to Kent Island and his land on the Eastern Shore were threatened in 1629 when George Calvert, 1st Lord Baltimore arrived at Jamestown, looking for the lands that his patron, King Charles I, had offered him. Virginia leaders, Claiborne among them, were worried about Lord Baltimore and his proposed Catholic colony. After returning to England Calvert decided to seek lands around the northern portion of the Chesapeake Bay. Indignantly, Claiborne went to London to try to block Lord Baltimore's proposed colony and to set up a fur-trading stock company to make Englishmen rich.

Claiborne sailed back to Virginia in 1631, but when he tried to create his fur-trading station at Kent Island, a disgruntled employee burned the warehouses of furs.

The long-sought-afte charter for the Calvert colony (Maryland) finally arrived from King Charles I in June, 1632, two months after the death of the first Lord Baltimore. In 1633, Claiborne fortified Kent Island and forcefully resisted Maryland's claims to it until 1637. During those years, he married and fathered his first child. When he returned to England in 1637 to again contest the Calvert land claims, his Kent Island plantation was burned by Marylanders, and his slaves and servants were hanged or seized.

Finally shut out of Kent Island, William Claiborne returned to Hampton and acquired 700 acres at Buckroe in Elizabeth City County and 3,000 acres on the Northern Neck of Virginia, near the Potomac. When Sir William Berkeley succeeded Sir Francis Wyatt as Virginia's governor in 1642, he named Claiborne as lifetime treasurer of the colony. In 1644, Claiborne led Virginia's militia against the Powhatan Indians after their second insurrection, forcing them off the Lower Peninsula.

When Oliver Cromwell became Lord Protector in England in 1653, having triumphed in his civil war against King Charles I, Berkeley was replaced as Virginia's governor by Richard Bennett. Claiborne then was chosen secretary of state and deputy governor.

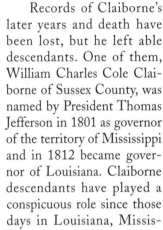

**First Lord Baltimore**

In 1653, the acquisitive fur-buyer acquired 5,000 more acres on the Pamunkey River near the present West Point, called the county New Kent and his new plantation, Romancoke. It was later inherited by Martha Custis, who married George Washington, and thus descended to John Parke Custis and his daughter, Mary, who became the wife of Robert E. Lee.

Records of Claiborne's later years and death have been lost, but he left able descendants. One of them, William Charles Cole Claiborne of Sussex County, was named by President Thomas Jefferson in 1801 as governor of the territory of Mississippi and in 1812 became governor of Louisiana. Claiborne descendants have played a conspicuous role since those days in Louisiana, Mississippi, and other states.

In the reconstructed 1639 church at Jamestown, a tablet today recalls the first William Claiborne as "Council Member, Treasurer, Deputy Governor, and Commander Against the Indians." The citation could have said a lot more.

Had it not been for Lord Baltimore's creation of Maryland, William Claiborne might have made Kent Island the center of a great fur-trading syndicate, buying up pelts traded throughout the colonies from Indians in exchange for food, clothing, and whiskey and sending furs to Great Britain to make coats and beaver hats, then in great demand. Today, Kent Island is a residential area.

In Hampton, William Claiborne was remembered for many years downtown because a building bore his name. But like those of most well-known pioneer Hampton families —Westwoods, Wythes, Keiths, Kirbys, Cockes—the family name has largely disappeared from the Peninsula, and the building now has been torn down.

# 3 Tobacco Fleet

FOREIGN PRIVATEERS and pirates, beginning twenty or thirty years after the settlement of Jamestown through the coming of the American Revolution, raided shipping and forced Great Britain and the colony of Virginia to develop a safer method of transporting products, chiefly tobacco, from Hampton Roads to British ports. The result was the tobacco fleet.

In those days, Hampton was the primary Virginia seaport, and commercial ships provided the linkage between Virginia and such British ports as London, Bristol, Plymouth, Liverpool, Aberdeen, and Glasgow. Large convoys of tobacco ships sailed from Hampton Roads each fall and spring, carrying hogsheads of cured "Orinoco" and "Sweet-Scented" leaf to British buyers.

In his book, *Tobacco Coast*, A. Pierce Middleton details the operations of the Virginia and Maryland tobacco fleets. The dates of the annual departure of "the fall fleet" and "the spring fleet" were posted at various courthouses, taverns, and church doors well in advance so Tidewater tobacco planters could load their hogsheads—each marked with the name of the sender and of his agent in Britain—in time to be loaded by ship and carried to an anchorage inside the capes.

*The British Museum*

**Typical tobacco fleet merchant vessel**

Virginia's coast was made to order for international trade in those days of shallow-draft ships. As one anonymous eighteenth-century writer put it in *The London Magazine*, July 1746, "'Tis the blessing of this country [Virginia] ... and fits it extremely for the trade it carries on, that the planters can deliver their commodities at their own back doors, as the whole colony is inter-flowed by the most navigable rivers in the world."

Hugh Jones, a former College of William and Mary professor, wrote in London in 1724 in his book *The Present State of Virginia*: "No country is better watered for the conveniency of which most houses are built near some landing place; so that anything may be delivered to a gentleman there from London, Bristol, etc."

The fleet concept was developed because, unfortunately, many tobacco ships never reached Great Britain. Although many sank during storms, the primary reason for the gathering of groups of ships was the problem of perennial attacks by Dutch or French privateers—fair game in the countless wars that divided Europe in those years.

And then there were pirates, who periodically lurked near Cape Charles to attack unescorted merchantmen. The most notorious

A cartouche depicts hogsheads being inspected prior to shipment overseas

was Blackbeard, who terrorized the capes for months in 1717 before he was killed and his ship and crew seized by two British men-of-war at Ocracoke.

Using Hampton as a base, British warships were anchored nearby to watch over the lower Chesapeake Bay while the cargos were accumulated and the ships loaded, often on smaller shallow draft boats, which took the hogsheads and other products out to the larger oceangoing vessels. The job of the warships then was to escort the tobacco fleet across the seas.

Once a tobacco fleet reached Great Britain and its cargo was sold by consignees, the ships were loaded with goods ordered by planters and with other goods from British manufacturers for sale in the colonies. Early ads in Williamsburg's *Virginia Gazette* often list commodities newly received from Britain and for sale.

Most ships returned via the Azores or Canary Islands, to take on fresh drinking water there and then return via the Caribbean to Hampton Roads. In this three-cornered trade, returning ships in the Caribbean were often loaded up with slaves, sugar, rum, and salt for

transport to Virginia. Therefore, it is easy to think today of the triangle trade as simply as "Tobacco to Rum to Slaves."

Virginia's ships were small by today's standards, often sailed by a crew of fewer than a dozen men, most of them slaves. Planters had their ships built in small boatyards on Tidewater's rivers. These smaller Virginia ships traded only with the Caribbean Islands, where their tobacco was reloaded on larger oceangoing vessels—that is, if the planters did not

Transporting tobacco hogsheads

**Hogsheads of tobacco are loaded into a ship bound for England**

want to send their products directly to England.

Bristol vied with London as Virginia's chief tobacco customer until 1685, to be replaced by Glasgow. In all their trade, Virginians sent many other products along with tobacco: corn, wheat, flour, iron, lumber, barrel staves, tar, pitch, and salted pork.

The goods came to the ports; those upriver were loaded to be taken to Hampton Roads, where they were transferred to large vessels. There the ships of the tobacco fleet waited for the appointed date to hoist sail and begin their voyage.

Sometimes there were as many as two hundred ships in the fleet, but mostly they averaged between fifty and eighty ships that followed the designated admiral on his British warship out into the Atlantic. Another British warship, following the convoy to ward off pirates and foreign attackers.

Later, in the eighteenth century, the biggest vessels were owned by Scottish merchants who prospered in Norfolk, Portsmouth, Petersburg, and Alexandria. Others were owned by major planters, individually or as partners. Among the owners were Washingtons, Carters, Byrds, Harrisons, Custises, Braxtons, and Fitzhughs. The tobacco fleets were rarely used by then, because most of the privateers and pirates had been put down.

# 4 When Pirates Roamed

IN COLONIAL TIMES, piracy flourished in Chesapeake Bay and along Atlantic sea-lanes that tobacco ships from the colony of Virginia traveled.

To combat the pirates, Great Britain dispatched a succession of patrol vessels to what is now Hampton Roads. Most of the seventeenth-century patrols operated out of Hampton, Virginia's major port from Jamestown's day until just before the American Revolution.

A reminder of those days remains in the name of Blackbeard's Point on Hampton's waterfront, where the bloody and bearded head of the bay's most notorious pirate was hung up to public view in 1717.

Another relic of Hampton's efforts against piracy is the little-known tomb in the deserted graveyard of Hampton's early Pembroke church, close to Interstate 64 and to the Hampton University campus. It is the eroded and now-illegible tombstone of Peter Hayman, who was collector of customs for the lower James River district in the year 1700. Since the James River district was then considered to encompass what later was named Hampton Roads, the lower James customs office was located at Hampton.

History and Lives of the Most Notorious Pirates, *1743*

**Pirates sometimes attacked a vessel anchored near a harbor**

The eroded Pembroke Church tombstone once contained this tantalizing inscription:

> In memory of Peter Heyman, Esq., grandson of Sir Peter Heyman of Summerfield in the County of Kent (England). He was Collector of Customs in the lower district of James River and went voluntarily on board the King's ship *Shoreham* in pursuit of a pirate who greatly infested this coast. After he had behaved himself seven hours with undaunted courage, was killed with a small shot the 29th day of April, 1700. In the engagement he stood next the Governor, upon the quarterdeck, and was here honorably interred by his order.

Behind that eroded tombstone is a heroic incident forgotten by all but a few history buffs.

It began with an outburst of piracy in the lower Chesapeake in the 1680s. Small, fast pirate ships, operated by crews of renegades from the Caribbean islands, hid out in the creeks and bays of the Eastern Shore, watching out for ships passing through the capes.

A General History of Pyrates, *1734*

**Pirate vessel battles merchant ship**

Whenever they saw an unescorted merchant vessel, the pirates would sail out and demand its surrender. If the merchant captain resisted, the pirates would open fire to dismast and disable the vessel, then board it and capture its cargo.

In 1684, during the governorship of Lord Howard of Effingham, the governor dispatched a ketch, HMS *Quaker*, to circuit the Chesapeake Bay and drive off buccaneers. Three pirate captains were caught in the James River in 1688 and sent to England for trial. Ultimately, the *Quaker* proved too small and too slow, so a larger ship, HMS *Shoreham*, was sent from England in 1700. She had only twenty-eight guns and 120 men, but she was big enough to attack pirate Louis Guittar's ship, *La Paix*, that April.

The *Shoreham* had just arrived for duty, working out of Hampton, when notorious Caribbean pirate Louis Guittar sailed into the capes. After plundering and destroying five small vessels, Guittar was surprised to see the *Shoreham* bearing down on him. He didn't know it, but Lieutenant Governor Francis Nicholson was aboard her, along with Peter Heyman, Hampton's collector of customs. As commander of Virginia's army and navy, Lieutenant Governor Nicholson "was anxious to arrest Guittar."

In the daylong battle, thirty-nine pirates were killed by the British guns. When *La Paix*'s sails and lines had been shattered by gunfire, the pirate ship was run aground and forced to surrender. Of one hundred pirates captured, three were hanged in Virginia and the rest sent to prison in England. Peter Heyman was the only man aboard the *Shoreham* known to have been killed.

The Reverend James Blair of Jamestown, who was then in England to urge King William and Queen Mary to create a college in Virginia, persuaded the government to give one-fourth of the pirate loot—a sizable amount—to help build the college.

Redoubling his efforts against

piracy, Governor Nicholson that spring ordered the militia of Elizabeth City, Princess Anne, Norfolk, Northampton, and Accomack counties to station lookouts along their coast. They stayed on duty until that fall, when 300 Virginia and Maryland tobacco ships had safely gathered in the bay, then sailed in convoy to England.

After Britain went to war with France in 1702, Virginia shippers faced the added threat of French warships and privateers. The House of Burgesses in Williamsburg petitioned England to send more naval ships, but because of the British Isles' wartime needs, the mother country could spare only a few vessels for the Chesapeake.

Alarm spread through the colony again in 1709 when a French privateer fleet was rumored to be entering the bay to capture black slaves and other "good booty." The Virginia militia was again called up, cannons were placed around the lower bay shoreline to fire warnings, and lookouts were again posted at strategic points. But the privateers failed to show up.

So dangerous were the sea-lanes from Virginia to England in those days that many Virginians forswore trips to the homeland. Virginia ships that traveled in convoy had to fly the English ensign at all times and fire a gun in case of danger to alert the other vessels. The naval officer commanding the lead convoy was designated as admiral, with another designated as rear admiral behind the convoy.

The Pirates Own Book, *1837*

**Pirate crew boards victim vessel during battle**

# 5 The Pirate Blackbeard

ONE OF HAMPTON'S earliest claims to fame was the fact that the head of Blackbeard, the devious and illustrious pirate who was killed by a British naval officer after a grueling fight, was hung on a pole near the entrance to Hampton River.

*Lives of Highwaymen and Pirates, 1736*
**Edward Teach, better known as Blackbeard**

The site is now known as Blackbeard's Point.

In fact, Blackbeard's Point is one of Hampton's oldest place names, dating from 1719. That was the year British sailors returned to Virginia after defeating Blackbeard's ragamuffins off Ocracoke Island on North Carolina's Outer Banks.

The sailors had been dispatched by Virginia Governor Alexander Spotswood, who wanted to end piracy by lawless brigands who attacked merchant ships trading between Virginia and the British Isles. Soon after he became governor in 1710, Spotswood stationed a small British warship, HMS *Pearl*, on guard duty in the lower Chesapeake Bay.

The most feared of all the pirates was Edward Teach, whose name was often written as *Tach, Thach, Thatch, Teatch*, or *Teach*. Wearing a beard that streamed from his cheeks to his waist, earning him the name "Blackbeard," he weighed about 250 pounds and stood nearly six feet, four inches—a giant of a man with a deep bass voice that often roared like a cannon.

Going into battle, wrote one witness, "he wore a sling over his shoulders, with three braces of pistols hanging in holsters [like bandoliers]. He then stuck lighted matches under his hat which, 'appearing on each side of his face, his eyes naturally looking fierce and wild, made him altogether such a figure that imagination cannot form an idea of a Fury from Hell to look more frightful.'"

Confirming the illusion, victims recounted Blackbeard saying, "I come from Hell and will carry you there presently unless you give me your money."

Some say Teach was an Englishman born in the home country. Others, however, say his surname was Drummond, and that he was born in Accomack. North Carolina author and historian Kevin P. Duffus has conducted years of research and genealogical investigations. He believes that Blackbeard was a Carolinian and that many of his crew were from around Bath, North Carolina.

In fact, Duffus, in his book *The Last Days of Black Beard the Pirate*, recounts that the scoundrel was really Edward Beard, the son of Captain James Beard of Goose

The Pirates Own Book, *1837*

**Maynard killed Blackbeard in 1718**

Creek near Charleston, South Carolina. Born near Charleston, Beard and his family later moved to Bath, where they had large land holdings.

Duffus believes that "Black" was a nickname, like other pirates used "Red" and "Black," and that Teach was an alias. He added that the surnames of numerous families in the Bath area match the names of some of Blackbeard's crew.

There also is a legend that his family owned a mansion across Hampton River where his head was finally displayed "as a trophy."

For years, Blackbeard plied his trade in the Caribbean. Charlotte Amalie in the Virgin Islands became a favorite haunt where he lay in wait for Spanish galleons. He became a wealthy man whose treasure rooms were filled with "great chests brimming with jewels, bars of gold and silver stacked like cordwood, and leather bags bulging with doubloons."

Later he moved his headquarters into the Bahama Islands where he continued to loot and pillage. Blackbeard is thought to have come to the Chesapeake Bay from the Caribbean in early 1717. His speedy sailing craft hid in coves near Cape Charles, only to dart out when he spied a merchant ship in the channel and to close on it with guns firing. Overcoming his prey, Blackbeard would loot the captured vessel of its money and valuable cargo and then sail away.

At that time, Blackbeard had joined forces with the "gentleman" pirate—Stede Bonnet—and within a short time had taken over Bonnet's ship and was in command of the entire operation. While awaiting his victims, Blackbeard hid in inlets along the Eastern Shore, thus evading a host of British and colonial naval sentries. He returned to the Caribbean in the fall.

Sailing northward again after a successful winter in the southern climate, Blackbeard found himself off the North Carolina coast. Hearing of grants of immunity available from Governor Charles Eden of North Carolina, Blackbeard went to Bath and surrendered and later created a "very good understanding" with Eden, who was in awe of the pirate and let him do as he wanted. The pirate even married a 16-year-old Bath girl, who joined his list of at least twelve other wives.

By summer of 1718, Blackbeard sailed back to the Bahamas and, en route, captured several vessels, including two French ships. He brought the booty back to Bath and received accolades from the governor, who allowed him to keep much of the treasure. For the next several months, he continued to plunder small vessels in the two Carolina sounds.

Alarmed at the continued piracy, Governor Spotswood dispatched two British sloops from the Chesapeake to the Outer Banks to search for the pirate.

Commanding the *Jane*, one of two hired sloops, was young Lieutenant Robert Maynard. When he found Blackbeard's ship, he engaged the pirate fiercely. It appeared, however, that Maynard and his crew had been defeated.

There were few signs of life on his vessel when Blackbeard's crew boarded it. Soon, however, the British sailors, who had been waiting below, rushed onto the deck, and hand-to-hand fights erupted. After twelve of Maynard's sailors had been killed and twenty-two injured, Maynard finally backed Blackbeard into a corner. Maynard and his men inflicted two dozen sword wounds on the pirate. Blackbeard also was shot five times before he finally died.

Members of Maynard's crew then cut off Blackbeard's head as a war trophy and kept it safe until they came near Hampton when the head was nailed to the bowsprit of the pirate's own ship, *Adventure*, for the arrival at the Hampton wharf. Later, Blackbeard's gory head was erected at the entrance to the harbor. The grisly sight is said to have remained there several years.

Maynard delivered the fifteen members of Blackbeard's crew whom he had captured to Governor Spotswood in Williamsburg. They were put in the colonial jail and, after trial, thirteen of them were hanged. After Blackbeard, there were still pirates in the Chesapeake Bay, but they were fewer and less fierce. Nevertheless marauding ships called privateers continued to prey on peaceful commerce off the Virginia shore.

Blackbeard's story has fascinated people ever since. Captain Charles Johnson, whose identity has never been established, included an account of Blackbeard in his eighteenth-century work *A General History of Pyrates*. Some, including Duffus, believe that Johnson was really English author and journalist Daniel Defoe writing under a pseudonym. Benjamin Franklin, when he was a 12-year-old boy, composed a poem about Blackbeard. Hundreds of books have been written through the years about the pirate—and today the tale still lingers, often embellished, but rarely diminished.

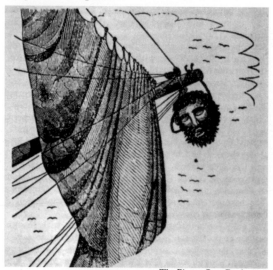

The Pirates Own Book, *1837*
**Blackbeard's head was hung from the ship's bowsprit**

# 6 First Free Public School

UP NORTH IN New England, the young "New College" was established in 1636 by the legislature of the Massachusetts Bay Colony. Two years later, in 1638, a young clergyman, John Harvard, died and left his library and half of his estate to the fledgling school. It was not, however, the earliest bequest to education in the American colonies.

That had come four years earlier in Virginia when Benjamin Syms or Symmes, who was born in England about 1590, left 200 acres on the Poquoson River situated in Elizabeth City County (now Hampton), along with "eight cows, a weeding hoe and some farm implements" for the establishment of a free school in Elizabeth City and "Kiquotan."

The free school district encompassed all the land from "Old Point up the Peninsula to Mary's Mount on the James and on the Poquoson River to the York or approximately where Harwood's Mill Reservoir is now situated."

Syms's will designated the justices of the peace of the county, the minister, and church wardens of Elizabeth City Parish (and their successors) as trustees of his endowment for the free school. The gift was approved in March 1642/43 by the Virginia House of Burgesses.

The Burgesses' resolution stated:

> Be it enacted and confirmed, upon consideration had of the godly disposition and good intent of Benjamin Syms deceased, in founding by his last will and testament a free school in Elizabeth county, for the encouragement of all others in like pious performances, that the said will and testament with all donations therein contained concerning the free school and the situation thereof in the said county, and the land appertaining to the same, shall be confirmed according to the godly intent of the said testator, without any alienation or conversion thereof to any place or county.

No records exist as to when the free school

*Hampton History Museum*

**The Hampton Academy was the successor to the Syms and Eaton schools**

was formally established, but by 1647 it is believed Syms School was operational because Syms's will (dated February 10, 1634/35) specifically required that upon the increase of the cattle "some part of them be sold for the erecting of a very sufficient school house." The rest of the increase of the herd would be sold later to provide funds for the maintenance of "the said School."

By the way, in 1647, it was recorded that the milk herd

*Hampton History Museum*
**Syms-Eaton Academy, circa 1842**

numbered forty cows and that there was a [school]house on the property. It is said that the boys "studied in the room on the left and the girls in the room on the right. The boys played in the front yard while the girls were required to stay in the back yard."

Ironically, another bequest in 1659 by a physician in the area resulted in the establishment of another free school. Thomas Eaton's will stipulated that five hundred acres of land on Back River, including "all houses, edifices, orchards, and Rights to it" and additionally two slaves, twelve cows and two bulls, twenty hogs, and an array of household furniture including milk pails and watering tubs, would go toward the establishment of his "free school." Like Syms, he also appointed trustees to supervise the will and subsequently the school.

Little is known about these schools through the years, but Lyon G. Tyler, president of the College of William and Mary, wrote in 1897 in his *William and Mary College Quarterly Historical Magazine* of records found between 1692 and 1699 that made mention of the two schools—Syms and Eaton.

For example, on November 20, 1693, the trustees apparently ordered a Robert Crook, schoolmaster of Syms School, to be paid for repairs to the schoolhouse and that two cows be sold to obtain money for the payment.

Also, on November 18, 1697, Mr. George Eland of the local court was elected the schoolmaster of Eaton's Charity School "and he to continue in place as he shall be approved of from year to year teaching all such children (from Elizabeth City County) in English and gramer learninge."

Acknowledging these Hampton schools as well as others throughout the Virginia colony, Robert Beverley Jr., a plantation owner known more for his historical work, in 1705, wrote in his *History and Present State of Virginia*:

> There are large tracts of land, houses, and other things granted to free schools for the education of children in many parts of this country. These schools have been founded by the legacies of well-inclined gentlemen, and the management of them hath commonly been left to the direction of the county court or the vestry of their respective parishes.

In an effort to help give more legal authority to the trustees of the two schools, the legislature gave incorporation powers to the trustees of both schools—Syms Free School in 1753 and Eaton Charity School in 1759. Tyler wrote in his historical magazine,

> The trustees were empowered to have perpetual succession; to use a corporate seal; to select and remove the master, who, before selection, was to be approved by the minister and by the governor; to visit the school; to order, reform, and redress all abuses; and to lease the school lands and the cattle thereon for a period not exceeding twenty-one years.

The *Virginia Gazette* carried an advertisement in 1752 that the "perquisites of Syms' school" was £31 annually. The act of 1759 testified to the good work performed by the Eaton school, to which, in addition to the proper objects of charity, "a great number of children" had been admitted free "who were able to pay for their own education." Thus, the school had to return to its original intent—free education for the poorer children.

The two schools, located since their beginnings in the "country," were difficult for children in the town of Hampton to attend. Citizens urged a consolidation, and a petition was sent to the Virginia General Assembly in 1803 asking for the change. A merger of the schools was effected by legislation two years later. The names of Syms and Eaton were eliminated and the new school—built in town on Cary Street—was called Hampton Academy.

The country folk and city residents argued for years about the location of the school, but finally in 1837 the Academy was the public school in Elizabeth City County. The Academy became part of the public education system in 1852 and continued for many years. The original building was burned in 1861 during the Civil War in the fire that destroyed much of the town. It was replaced, and in 1902 yet another structure, a brick building, was built on the original site and the name was eliminated—and Syms-Eaton Academy was born.

Today, Hampton High School is the successor to the Syms and Eaton schools with its original building, in fact, on the old Hampton Academy (Syms-Eaton) grounds. A newer high school was built in 1922 on Victoria Boulevard. Two middle schools now honor Thomas Eaton and Benjamin Syms, original seventeenth-century benefactors of education in the area. Interest from the money set aside in those two trusts centuries ago is still being used to further education in Hampton today.

*Hampton History Museum*

**Syms-Eaton Academy (elementary school) opened on February 13, 1902**

# 7 St. John's Church Survives

**M**EDIEVAL EUROPEAN cities prided themselves on their cathedrals, and early Virginia towns took similar pride in their Anglican churches. One of them was St. John's Episcopal Church in Hampton, the brick edifice on Queen Street that is the fourth church of Elizabeth City Parish—the oldest Anglican parish in continuous existence in America.

St. John's, built in 1728, was damaged by the British in the Revolutionary War and the War of 1812, and it was nearly ruined when Hampton was burned in 1861. But each time, the proud congregation rebuilt it.

The location of the first church in Elizabeth City Parish is near present-day LaSalle and Chesapeake avenues, according to archaeological excavations. Tradition has it that services of the parish were held at Kecoughtan. The bishop of London appointed the Reverend William Mease as the first minister to lead the church at Kecoughtan. He served from 1610 to 1620.

The second church stood on the east side of Hampton River, where the settlement had been reestablished by 1623. That site is now surrounded by the campus of Hampton University, where the foundations were discovered about 1910. Archaeologists uncovered the original foundations for the wooden structure, and some of the tile floor was also revealed. Surviving from the second church and still in use is the 1628 communion silver, the oldest in continuous use anywhere in English-speaking America.

The third church of 1667—located just a mile west of the second church—was also a rectangular wooden structure. The site was called Westwoods Town Quarter. It is east of LaSalle Avenue just off West Pembroke Avenue. Some seventeenth- and eighteenth-century tombstones have been found at the site, and bricks outline the old building.

By 1728, when con-

Frank Leslie's Illustrated Newspaper, *August 17, 1861*

**St. John's Church, completed by 1728, added a belfry in 1762**

struction of the present St. John's was completed, Virginia was becoming prosperous from tobacco exports. Many handsome Tidewater churches were built in that era. The exterior walls are of Flemish bond with glazed headers, and the colonial window arches and jambs are of rubbed brick.

It is believed that Henry Cary Jr. of Williamsburg completed construction on the cruciform building. He earlier had built The Brafferton and several years later, the President's House, on the College of William and Mary campus. In 1762 the church belfry was added.

Like all early Anglican churches in Virginia, St. John's was hard hit by the disestablishment of Anglicanism (as the official state church in Virginia) following the American Revolution and by the subsequent rise of Baptists and Methodists and other popular denominations.

After St. John's was damaged when Hampton was partially burned by Admiral Sir George Cockburn's British invaders in 1813, the old church fell into ruin and disuse. But after Bishop Richard Channing Moore rallied the Episcopal Church in Virginia, Hampton's parish church was repaired in 1827 and reconsecrated in 1830 and given the name St. John's.

An old print of this period shows the church looking much like today's Bruton Parish Church in Williamsburg, with a handsome bell tower and with a weeping willow shading its churchyard.

By 1861, when Virginia seceded from the Union, Hampton was a town of some two thousand residents. Because it was near the powerful Union base of Fort Monroe, Hampton was evacuated, and Confederate General John Bankhead Magruder ordered his troops to burn their own houses, businesses, and even the church. August 7, 1861, was Hampton's worst day.

"The fire was set so unexpectedly and burned so rapidly," wrote one observer, "that the

*Editor's Collection*
**Only the walls remained after the 1861 fire**

residents were forced to flee with empty hands. Many felt that the abandoned portraits of their loved ones were the severest loss."

After the fire, little except the brick walls of St. John's remained. One witness wrote, "Old Hampton lies in ruins, every house being consumed ... but the naked walls of 500 houses remain like skeletons, giving us some faint idea of the beauty, wealth and enjoyment of the past."

A Union soldier who marched through Hampton in 1862 with General George B. McClellan's invading Army of the Potomac, wrote:

We pitched our tents amid the charred and blackened ruins of what had been the beautiful and aristocratic village of Hampton. The only building left standing ... was the massive old Episcopal church.

**Visitor card for St. John's, circa 1920, with schedule**

St. John's Church, Hampton, Va.
Elizabeth City Parish.
"Oldest Continuous Church in America."
Established in 1610.

| | |
|---|---|
| First visited by the English | May 10, 1607 |
| Settled by Lord DeLa Warr | July, 1610 |
| Reinforced by Sir Thomas Dale | May, 1611 |
| First Church erected | 1620 |
| Present Church, third in the Parish, erected | 1727 |
| Town and Church sacked | Jan. 24-27, 1813 |
| Church repaired | 1827 |
| Consecrated by Bishop Moore | Jan. 8, 1830 |
| Town and Church burned | Aug. 7-8, 1861 |
| Original walls stood and the Church restored | 1868-1870 |

**SERVICES.**

SUNDAYS
8:45 A. M.   Holy Communion.
9:30 A. M.   Church School.
11:00 A. M.   Morning Prayer and Sermon.
11:00 A. M.   Holy Communion and Sermon.
 (First Sunday in the month)
7:30 P. M.   Evening Prayer and Sermon.
HOLY DAYS
10:00 A. M.   Holy Communion.

Baptism by appointment.
The Rector and clergy of St. John's are at the service of any persons to whom they can be of help. All seats in St. John's Church are free.

Many makeshift dwellings were built along the streets, some housing freed blacks who flocked to Fort Monroe in 1863 after President Abraham Lincoln announced his Emancipation Proclamation. These homes were gradually replaced during Reconstruction as new residents came to town. Many former Union soldiers who had served in Virginia during the war returned to live after 1865. They and their descendants were called "65ers" by old Hamptonians.

In 1869, when the parishioners of St. John's rebuilt their church for a second time on the site, they Victorianized the once-colonial structure. Its plain windows were replaced with stained glass biblical scenes—popular at the time—and its interior was in the Victorian style with white walls and a ceiling of open timbers. And the ruined belfry was removed. One of the stained glass windows, illustrating Indian princess Pocahontas, was given in part by Indian students from the Hampton Normal and Agricultural Institute (now Hampton University). Those students, in 1887 at the time of the gift, worshiped at the church.

Church records indicate that a rear tower was added early in the twentieth century, a tracker organ installed in 1981, and a chapel constructed a few years later.

St. John's churchyard was Hampton's principal cemetery for many years and boasts some of the oldest gravestones on the Peninsula. It is still being used. Many men and women who have made Hampton history are buried there —Westwoods, Kirbys, Phillipses, Sinclairs, Mallorys, Phoebuses, Groomes, Darlings, Holts, and others.

# 8 George Wythe, "Legal Brain"

COLONIAL LEGAL SCHOLAR and jurist George Wythe was born at Chesterville, his family's plantation in Elizabeth City County. After the Civil War, the county established three districts—one of them Wythe—to honor him. Today the Olde Wythe neighborhood in Hampton survives, maintaining the area's link to its celebrated patriot.

But is was on the Wythe family estate that George, the son of planter Thomas Wythe, came into the world in 1726, probably in an old stone house that stood on the property. His great-grand-father, Thomas Wythe I, purchased 204 acres of land in the area about 1691, according to records of the National Aeronautics and Space Administration's Langley center, which now encompasses the Chesterville site. After inheriting the plantation from his brother Thomas Wythe IV, George amassed about 1,050 acres by 1771.

It was his mother, Margaret Walker Wythe, who gave her son his early education and imbued him with his lifelong love of learning. Later he taught himself a variety of subjects, including Hebrew. Wythe learned law from his uncle Stephen Dewey, who practiced near Petersburg. Admitted to the bar in 1746, George practiced in his home county for many years, living at Chesterville from 1746 until about 1754. His first marriage in 1747, to young Ann Zachery, daughter of Wythe's law

*John A. Lanzalotti, M.D.*
**George Wythe**

mentor, ended with her death about a year later.

The House of Burgesses first included Wythe as a member in 1754 following his successful election from Williamsburg. He was elected in 1758 from the College of William and Mary and in 1761 from Elizabeth City County. In 1767, he was elected clerk of the House and remained in that position until his election to the Second Continental Congress in 1775.

At age 49, he was called a "classical scholar" and today would have been touted as a "legal brain." He joined an impressive array of intellectuals and colonial leaders, including Richard Henry Lee, Thomas Jefferson, Benjamin Harrison, Thomas Nelson Jr., Francis Lightfoot Lee, and Carter Braxton as Virginia delegates to that congress.

When the group ultimately signed Thomas Jefferson's Declaration of Independence in 1776, Wythe was away from Philadelphia. But the story goes that his colleagues so highly respected him that they left space so his signature would be first among the Virginians when he ultimately signed.

More than a decade later, Wythe was among another group of Virginians elected to help shape a nation. The Virginia delegation to the Constitutional Convention of 1787 included Wythe, Edmund Randolph, George Mason, James Madison, George Washington,

National Aeronautics and Space Administration
**Wythe's home, Chesterville, circa 1905**

In 1791, Wythe was appointed as judge of Virginia's Court of Chancery in Richmond. He died in June 1806 after being poisoned by his grandnephew, George Wythe Sweeney.

Jefferson, reflecting on Wythe's life, wrote:

> No man ever left behind him a character more venerated than George Wythe. His virtue was of the purest tint; his integrity inflexible, and his justice exact; of warm patriotism, and, devoted as he was to liberty, and the natural and equal rights of man, he might truly be called the Cato of his country.

A new plantation home was built by Wythe at Chesterville about 1771, when windows, nails, and hardware came from London for the house. Some architectural historians have suggested that Jefferson worked with Wythe on its design. Wythe continued to manage the property as a plantation until 1792. Three years later, he advertised the sale of Chesterville, including the home, kitchen, storehouse, granary, servants' quarters, stable, and a wharf. It was finally sold in 1802.

German immigrant and entrepreneur Francis A. Schmelz bought Chesterfield in 1875. He later gave it to his daughter Fannie, who lived there with her husband, Robert S. Hudgins, until 1911 when a kerosene kitchen stove exploded resulting in a fire that destroyed the home.

The *Daily Press* reported in its May 11, 1911, edition that "four massive blacked walls, surrounding a smoldering heap of debris, are all that remains of 'Chesterville,' the home of George Wythe," located in the Back River section about eight miles from Hampton. "The fire was fierce, and as the walls (four bricks thick) of the house refused to give to the heat, the time consumed eating the framework away was considerable."

In 1950, the Chesterville site became a part of National Advisory Council of Aeronautics, which in 1958 became National Aeronautics and Space Administration (NASA).

—*Wilford Kale*

John Blair II, and Dr. James McClurg, who also was born in Hampton and taught at William and Mary.

Only Washington, Madison, and Blair signed the document. Wythe strongly supported the document and would have been one of the few men to sign America's two seminal documents, but for the illness of his second wife, Elizabeth Taliaferro, which called him back to Williamsburg. Elizabeth Wythe, whose son Richard built the home on Palace Green now called the Wythe House, died a few months later.

Wythe, however, is probably better known as the law tutor of Thomas Jefferson and James Monroe. In 1779, he was named the first professor of law in the nation, joining the faculty at William and Mary where he remained until a 1789 dispute with college officials resulted in his resignation. Among his college students was the young John Marshall, who later became Chief Justice of the United States. Many law students also boarded with Wythe.

22  *HAMPTON IN THE BYGONE DAYS*

# 9 The American Revolution

THE SAGA OF HAMPTON in the American Revolution is much less known than that of the activities surrounding it during the later Civil War, but the community of about one thousand people possessed "the spirit of patriotic resistance" like many other Virginia localities.

Possibly the best account of Hampton in the Revolution can be found in Lyon G. Tyler's *History of Hampton and Elizabeth City County*, published by the county's board of supervisors in 1922.

In it, he listed the committee of safety formed on November 23, 1775, for the county and town of Hampton. A few months earlier Hampton was the location for the first real British encounter in the colony. It happened over runaway slaves and sailors who would land on the shore at night and carry off livestock and other goods before patriotic forces could be aroused.

However, on September 2, a hurricane appeared in Tidewater and forced the English sloop *Otter* to run aground at Hampton. The captain of the vessel was Mathew Squire, the leader of the night raids. Most of the sailors and officers managed to escape, but Squire became separated from his men and wandered the area all night until he

*National Galleries of Scotland*

**John Murray**

managed to get "friendly protection" from the fleet of John Murray, earl of Dunmore, the last royal governor of Virginia who had abandoned Williamsburg for the safety of Norfolk and Tidewater. Ultimately, he decided to stay aboard ship in Hampton Roads.

Later Squire demanded that officials of Hampton return his ship's stores which had been looted by townspeople during the storm. They agreed, Tyler wrote, on the condition that Squire "deliver up a Negro slave belonging to a Henry King" and cease his night forays. Squire, of course, would not agree and threatened violence.

Word of Squire's intention reached Williamsburg, still the colony's capital, where James Innis, captain of the Williamsburg Guard, decided to march his one hundred men to protect Hampton. When they arrived, Squire seemed quiet, and seeing no threat, Innis and his guard returned to Williamsburg.

To bolster Hampton's defenses, about a hundred other guardsmen were sent to encamp in the town's vicinity, where, on October 24, Squire decided to make a show of force. In the Hampton River came six armed tenders from Lord Dunmore's fleet with a warning they were going to land and burn the town. Captain George Nicholas and

An artist's drawing of the battle of Hampton

bombardments continued for quite a while, and many of the town's buildings, including St. John's Church, were injured by the fire from the British. After Squire's attack in 1775, there were no other assaults, but "the waters and countryside in the vicinity were the scenes of conflict at each invasion of the British." In 1780, ships commanded by Benedict Arnold came through the Virginia Capes into Hampton Roads and captured some small ships of the "Virginia navy." Sailors from the British vessels again made landing raids in and around Hampton to pillage and plunder.

The famous 1781 visit by Charles, Lord Cornwallis, to the Peninsula caused troops to once again forage through the area, including Hampton.

Tyler's narrative continues with a recitation of Hampton town heroes during the Revolution. High on the list was the eminent lawyer George Wythe, who was born outside Hampton at Chesterville on Back River. He later "attained almost equal distinction as a statesman, a jurist, and an interpreter of law, being the preceptor of both Thomas Jefferson and John Marshall," Tyler said.

his company of regulars and a small group of militias formed Hampton's defense.

British sailors attempted to land but were thwarted when they encountered boats that had been sunk in the river channel, another defensive maneuver.

Tyler wrote: "Squire then commanded a furious cannonade, and under that cover sent armed men in boats to make a landing, but the Virginians sent so many death shots that the boats were obliged to return."

Reinforcement arrived from Williamsburg, and the British tried another assault with cannons, which were returned "with a hot fire." The

Others included William Roscow; Wilson Curle, chairman of the county committee of safety, colonel of the county militia and later one of the first judges of the admiralty court established under the new Commonwealth of Virginia; Miles King, businessman, later mayor of Norfolk; and a naval leader, Captain Joseph Meredith.

# 10 The War of 1812

A BAD DAY IN HAMPTON'S history was June 25, 1813, when British forces under Admiral George Cockburn and General Sir Sydney Beckwith invaded the town and partly burned it. The attack was a prelude to the British burning of Washington, D.C., eighteen months later in the so-called War of 1812.

Oddly enough, Hampton histories say little about the invasion, although they remember the Confederate burning of their own town in 1861 during the Civil War in a vain attempt to keep it out of Yankee hands.

The 1813 invasion was Britain's revenge for its failure to burn Norfolk and Portsmouth a few days earlier—attempts frustrated by 10,000 Virginia militiamen on Craney Island and at Norfolk.

*19th-century engraving*
**George Cockburn**

The invasion led to Britain's two-year naval embargo of the Atlantic Coast, which stalled Virginia exports of tobacco and cotton. Only a few blockade runners and privateers got into Hampton Roads.

British depredations from the War of 1812 motivated the United States in the 1820s to build Fort Monroe, along with eleven other coast artillery forts along the Atlantic and Gulf of Mexico from Maine to New Orleans.

The Hampton invasion was described by historian Benson J. Lossing in his useful *Field Book of the War of 1812*, published years later.

By then, the British had apologized for their uncivilized warfare, but that didn't mollify Hamptonians who were not repaid for their ruined property.

But the experience had one benefit: It pushed the federal government to take steps to better defend the coast.

The heroes of Hampton were Virginia militiamen under Brigadier General Robert Barraud Taylor, a Norfolk lawyer whose family came from Williamsburg. The 10,000 civilian warriors were called up by Governor John Barbour in Richmond to defend the exposed port towns of Norfolk, Portsmouth, Hampton, and Suffolk.

The British sailed into Hampton Roads on

*Virginia Historical Society*
**Robert Barraud Taylor**

June 19, 1813, and anchored near Hampton and Old Point. They were rudely awakened at 4 a.m. the next morning by fourteen row-boats full of sailors from the naval shipyard at Portsmouth, who attacked one frigate in the dark. When other British ships joined in the battle, the Portsmouth fighters had to flee.

The attack on Norfolk began June 21 when twenty British men-of-war, frigates, and transports moved to the mouth of the Nansemond River near Craney Island and the Elizabeth

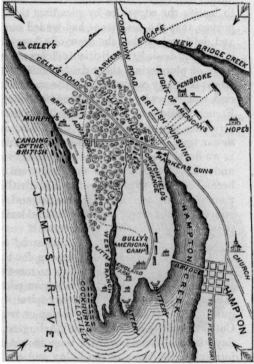

Benson J. Lossing, Pictorial Field Book of the Revolution, *1850*
**Plan of battle in Hampton area**

River near Norfolk. Their objective was Norfolk and Portsmouth. The chief American defense was a hastily built fort at the east end of Craney Island, equipped with two twenty-four-pound guns and one eighteen-pounder. It was manned by four hundred Virginia militiamen who knew their jobs.

Unbelievably, General Taylor and his Virginians were able to turn back the British fleet plus the hundreds of marines and French mercenaries aboard the British transports.

Wrote a Virginia militiaman, William P. Young of Craney Island:

While we were [hoisting the American flag], the enemy was landing his infantry and Marines, in all about 2,500. ... We knew not but their intention was to march to the town of Portsmouth ... and destroy the Navy yard. We were, however, soon undeceived.

When the British fired Congreve rockets into the Craney Island fort, the Americans returned fire. They killed two British officers and several men.

Then the Virginia defenders saw about fifty British landing barges coming ashore on Craney's seaward side, near the present Monitor-Merrimack Bridge Tunnel. The Virginians held their fire until Captain Arthur Emmerson, who commanded a Portsmouth artillery company, signaled "Fire." The first wave of Britons was badly hurt, and survivors were forced to retreat. Among those killed were French soldiers who had been captured by the British from Napoleon's troops in Spain.

According to Lossing, Britain's foremost casualties were Captain John Martin Hanchett, an illegitimate son of King George III and half-brother to his royal successors, George IV and William IV.

It was getting late, so the British abandoned their unrewarding attack. They turned in revenge on Hampton. The invasion began with the predawn landing of the troops near the home of Daniel Murphy, adjacent to Miles Cary's plantation. This put them near the present Newport News–Hampton city line. Hampton's defenders at first failed to spot the enemy, for they were misled by a feint by forty British boats toward Blackbeard's Point on Hampton River.

"The enemy landed and had drawn up in battle array at least 2,500 men," reported Hampton's commander, Major Stapleton Crutchfield, to Governor Barbour on June 28. They took full control of Hampton, burning, pillaging, and plundering stores.

It was a harsh invasion. The British commandeered Hampton's homes and demanded food from nearby plantations. They captured the American garrison at Old Point Comfort Lighthouse. Angered by their defeat at Craney

Island, their French-led soldiers indulged in rape and cruelty. After months of seagoing, the French soldiers, called "Chasseurs Britanniques," ran wild.

Major Crutchfield wrote:

> The unfortunate females of Hampton who could not leave the town were suffered to be abused in the most shameful manner, not only by the venal, savage foe but by unfortunate and infuriated blacks, who were encouraged in their success. They pillaged and encouraged every act of rapine and murder, killing a poor man by the name of Kirby, … shooting his wife in the hip at the same time, and killing his faithful dog.

General Taylor protested to Admiral Sir Boarlase Warren, commanding the British fleet aboard HMS *San Domingo*. Warren replied that the British were merely retaliating for American cruelty at Craney Island. Taylor appointed four of his officers to investigate the charge, but they found no American cruelty on Craney.

Later, Lieutenant Colonel Charles James Napier, who led some of the British invaders, confided to his diary that "Every horror was perpetrated [by the British] with impunity—rape, murder, pillage—and not a man was punished."

Except for Napier's diary, which did not come to light until later, the British never acknowledged misconduct at Hampton except for those eighteen French mercenaries. General Beckwith said he had ordered the French out of

town and back to their ship as soon as he learned of their misconduct. He blamed it on cruelties the French had encountered while fighting for Napoleon in Spain. "They could not be restrained," Beckwith said, lamely.

Admiral Cockburn and Beckwith moved into town to the house of Mr. and Mrs. John Westwood to run the occupation. Several of Hampton's houses then had windmills to grind wheat and corn, and these were stripped of their sails. The ancient communion silver of St. John's Church also was seized.

Writing to the *Richmond Enquirer* a few days later, Colonel Richard E. Parker of the Westmoreland Militia said,

> Hampton exhibits a dreary and desolate appearance which no American can witness unmoved. Men of Virginia! Will you permit all this? Fathers and brothers and husbands, will you fold your arms in apathy and only curse your despoilers? No!

Accounts of Hampton's conquest published in the Northern press identified the town as "Little Hampton," to distinguish it from the Hamptons on Long Island in New York.

The Hampton invasion infuriated Virginians and created widespread anti-British sentiment. Thomas Jefferson, James Madison, and James Monroe were strongly critical of His Majesty's government. "Remember Hampton!" remained a rallying cry. There were demands for more American soldiers and strong coastal defenses.

"Our force was altogether insufficient at Hampton," wrote Sergeant James Jarvis of Portsmouth. "Had our people been equal or two-thirds the number of the enemy, the Hamptonians would not have been compelled to retreat. They fought like heroes."

Finally the British withdrew, later to be heard from when they attacked and burned Washington, D.C. It took Hampton, Washington, and America years to recover.

*Benson J. Lossing,* Pictorial Field Book of the Revolution, *1850*
**British landing site and the ruins of Daniel Murphy's home**

# 11 Edgar Allan Poe at Monroe

O F ALL THE CHARACTERS to pass through Fort Monroe, none was more unmilitary than Edgar Allan Poe. Yet Poe spent a crucial four months at the post in the years 1828–1829, when he was 19, trying to become a soldier. From there he went on to the United States Military Academy at West Point, where he finally realized he was not cut out for the military.

Virginia claims Poe because he spent much of his life in Richmond as the foster son of John Allan, a wealthy tobacco shipper.

Actually, Poe was born in Boston in 1809, the son of an actor and actress —David Poe Jr. and Elizabeth Arnold Poe. When his mother died in Richmond three years later (she is buried in St. John's churchyard there), the little boy was given a home by the Allans.

But Poe was a moody, nervous, introverted, gloomy, and undisciplined boy, and his foster father never understood or loved him. Allan wanted the boy to be a businessman or lawyer, but the young Poe lived in an imaginary world, far removed from Richmond's tobacco markets, and spent his unhappy life trying to live on earnings as a poet and short-story writer, dealing with stories of mystery and the supernatural.

In the hard-working, youthful America of Poe's lifetime, there was little opportunity for

Daily Press *Archives*

**Edgar Allan Poe**

writers. He died early, at age 40, after a chaotic career—a genius never fully recognized in his lifetime.

The University of Virginia opened in 1825, and Allan sent the boy to the second session beginning February 14, 1826. He lived in Room 13 on the West Range. He passed his courses apparently with good grades, according to a brief biography by James Southall Wilson, but lost money gambling and came home, and Allan refused to allow him to return to school.

Poe quarreled with his foster father, and the 18-year-old youth fled Richmond for Boston, where a thin book of his writings, *Tamerlane and Other Poems*, was published in 1827; it sold only a few copies. In desperation, he enlisted in the army on May 26, 1827, under the assumed name of Edgar A. Perry, and was sent to Fort Moultrie, South Carolina. When he did well as an army clerk, he was promoted from private to "artificer," or mechanic, and on October 31, 1828, was promoted again to regimental sergeant major, the highest rank an enlisted man could reach in those days. He was then sent to Fort Monroe.

Young Poe arrived at Old Point on December 15, 1828, and served there with a good record until April 15 of the next year. He lived in barracks now gone, close to the casemates that still line Monroe's moat. But army life

28

Fort Monroe, seen from the "Rip Raps," near the time of Poe's last visit

bored him, and he tried in a series of letters to persuade John Allan in Richmond to let him leave the army.

"The period of an Enlistment is five years —the prime of my life would be wasted—I shall be driven to more decided measures if you refuse to assist me," he wrote Allan in December 1828. However, Allan did not reply. Again, on December 22, 1828, Poe wrote Allan, "All that is necessary to obtain my discharge from the Army was your consent in a letter to Lieut. J. Howard." Again, Poe got no reply.

A month later, Poe tried Allan again. This time, in a letter of February 4, 1829, he proposed that his foster father help him get out of the army to go to West Point. He said his experience as an enlisted man would help him sail through "the Point" with no trouble and become an officer. If he got no reply, Poe said, he would go into exile in a foreign land.

Poe's foster mother, Frances Valentine Allan, had been an understanding parent and had tried to soften her husband's attitude toward Poe. When she died suddenly in Richmond on February 28, 1829, Poe was invited by John Allan to come home. Softening a little, the foster father agreed to pay a substitute to finish out the rest of Poe's enlistment and also to help him get into West Point.

Accordingly, he was discharged at Monroe on April 15, 1829. For the sum of $75, Sergeant Samuel "Bully" Graves of Fort Monroe agreed to serve out the rest of Poe's enlistment. Poe's officers gave him glowing letters of recommendation, one writing that he was "highly worthy of confidence." Another said Poe's education was "of a very high order" and that he appeared to be "free of bad habits." He recommended the undisciplined youth for a cadetship without hesitation.

Even so, Poe had to wait more than a year before an opening occurred at West Point. During this time, he stayed in Richmond and Baltimore. Several of his letters to Fort Monroe colleagues survive in which he promises to repay money he owes to friends. (The Old Rock House in Richmond near Poe's home and workplace serves today as a Poe Museum and shrine.)

But Poe liked West Point no better than Fort Monroe. He entered on July 1, 1830, but cut classes and absented himself from drills from the start. It was clear his heart wasn't in a military career. After a court-martial, he was dismissed on March 6, 1831, angering John Allan again.

Once out of West Point, though, Poe demonstrated briefly the tremendous talent he was striving to put to use. He wrote "The Raven" and other fine poems, and he became

*Casemate Museum Collection*

**An artist's depiction of Poe as an enlisted man at Fort Monroe**

Hampton's Mill Creek and facing Chesapeake Bay.

An old Casemate Museum publication at Fort Monroe paints a romantic picture of Poe's visit there:

> The onetime enlisted man, now world-famous, could hear Fort Monroe bugle calls floating over the walls of the massive fort (behind the hotel). He heard the boom of the evening gun. This must have recalled to the 40-year-old Poe memories of his youth, when all life stretched before him. That evening (at the request of admirers) Poe recited his poetry on the hotel veranda in the moonlight.

Besides "The Raven" and "Annabel Lee," Poe recited the mystical "Ulalume," explaining that the last stanza of "Ulalume" might not be intelligible to listeners because he scarcely understood it himself. A young girl praised it, and Poe sent her a manuscript copy of the poem.

He wrote his admirer, who was Susan Ingram of Norfolk, "I have transcribed 'Ulalume' with much pleasure, Dear Miss Ingram—as I am sure I would do anything else at your bidding—but I fear that you will find the verses scarcely more intelligible today in my manuscript than last night in my recitation." He went on to Norfolk from Old Point for further lectures.

The last weeks of Poe's tragic life are clouded in uncertainty. Where had he gone, what had he done, after his visit to Old Point and Norfolk? All we know is that on October 3, he was picked up in a coma on a street in Baltimore. He died in delirium on October 7, 1849, just four weeks after his Old Point visit.

Poe's last words were "God help my poor soul."

editor of the *Southern Literary Messenger* in Richmond. For a while, he was able to support his young wife, Virginia Clemm, his cousin whom he married in 1836. But Virginia's death in 1847 led to new agonies and excesses that drove Poe further into debt and discredit.

Poe came back Fort Monroe for the last time—about twenty years after he left. He spent September 9, 1849, at the beautiful old Hygeia Hotel, which had been built by the Armistead family to house visitors and newly arrived servicemen at Monroe. The event must have brought back strong memories of his youthful service, when the big fort had been under construction adjoining

# 12 "Rip Raps," Presidential Retreat

THE FIVE-ACRE "Rip Raps," adjoining the Hampton Roads Bridge-Tunnel, has been called the most expensive wasteland in Virginia. From the time the army began creating the artificial island on a sandy shoal between Fort Monroe and the Norfolk shore, it managed to spend well over $3 million on it.

The island was abandoned by the federal government and reverted to the Commonwealth of Virginia in 1967. Today, it is visited by summertime tour boats and can be seen as one crosses Hampton Roads on the bridge-tunnel now linked to it.

"Rip Raps" is the nickname for the small fortification that from 1819 until 1862 was called "Castle Calhoun" or Fort Calhoun, for Secretary of War John C. Calhoun of South Carolina, and later was renamed Fort Wool, honoring a Fort Monroe commander.

The small island bears ruins of earlier construction and sparse vegetation. It is hard to believe that President John Tyler would have gone there from the White House for a while in 1842 to seek solace after the death of his first wife, the former Letitia Christian of Charles City County.

Actually, though, the dusty island has known a lot of famous visitors. Second Lieutenant Robert E. Lee of the Army Corps of Engineers helped build it while he was stationed at Fort Monroe from 1831 to 1834.

President Andrew Jackson spent a few weeks in a "summer White House" on the island on several occasions in 1829, 1831, 1833 and 1835.

Jackson's first visit to the area, July 9–11, 1829, came just four months after his inauguration. During the trip to the Rip Raps, the president seemed very pleased with the construction work on the small artificial island. About six weeks later, in late August, according to Colonel Robert Arthur's book, *Defender of the Chesapeake—The Story of Fort Monroe*, Jackson returned and stayed on Rip Raps

*Casemate Museum Collection*

"Rip Raps," a man-made island off Fort Monroe

rather than at Fort Monroe. A grocery bill for the ten-day retreat reportedly included veal, steak, ducks, turtle soup, English cheese and a gallon of whiskey.

In its September 1, 1829 edition, *The Richmond Enquirer* said Jackson had been "inhaling the salubrious ocean breeze and daily taking a salt water bath." The newspaper reported that the president "is at all times accessible and affable to those who call on him merely en passant, and appears to enjoy a fine flow of spirits."

Jackson so much enjoyed the Rip Raps that he returned in June 1831 and again in July 1833. "His hotel at the Rip Raps is a delightful summer residence, freely inviting the breeze over the waters from every point of the compass, and with the polite and attentive host of the Hygeia, Mr. Marshall Parks, to cater for this table, he cannot be otherwise than 'comfortable,'" Colonel Arthur wrote. The *Norfolk Herald* reported that Jackson declined a visit to Norfolk that August in order "to remain free from bustle and fatigue."

In 1842, President Tyler, a Virginian, was the next chief executive to use Rip Raps, or Fort Calhoun. Following the death of his first wife and her interment in Charles City County, Tyler boarded a steamer near Jamestown and came to Old Point Comfort. He stayed for many days in mourning.

Two years later, following his wedding to Julia Gardiner, daughter of United States Senator David Gardiner of New York, Tyler and his bride came to Fort Monroe for part of their honeymoon. It is quite possible that the couple also visited Rip Raps during their stay. Then in 1845, several months after retiring from the presidency, the Tylers returned for their first wedding anniversary.

*Editor's collection*
**President Andrew Jackson**

*Library of Congress*
**President John Tyler**

The quarters on the Rip Raps where the two presidents had lived burned in 1846 and were not replaced. (Tyler apparently liked the area so much that he purchased a Hampton home, called "The Villa," which the family used at least until the Civil War.)

President Abraham Lincoln came to Fort Monroe on May 8, 1862, a few days after General George B. McClellan and his huge Army of the Potomac had captured Williamsburg at the start of the Peninsula campaign. Lincoln inspected the new guns erected on the tiny island. The next day he returned to Rip Raps to observe the bombardment of the Confederate fortifications at Sewell's Point, which the Federals took a day or so later.

Today, only eight casemates from that era survive on the oyster-shaped island. Its principal military use in World War I and World War II was to anchor a submarine net across the main Hampton Roads channel leading to the James River.

The artificial island was conceived in 1818 by Brigadier General Simon Bernard, a French engineer engaged by the U.S. Army to plan Fort Monroe and a series of other Atlantic and Gulf Coast forts, authorized to prevent a repetition of the British naval depredations of the United States in the War of 1812. As a subsidiary of Fort Monroe, the Rip Raps was a part of the defense of Hampton Roads, and enabled in wartime the anchoring of a log-boom between the two shores to prevent enemy vessels from entering the channel.

But Fort Calhoun (its official name) seemed doomed from the start. Tons of granite blocks brought from out of state on scows were dropped onto the shallow shoal, only to sink into the sandy bottom of Hampton Roads. By the end of 1819, only four percent of the vast

Buildings and cranes on the "Rip Raps," circa 1860

amount of stone poured into the ten-foot-deep shoal showed above water. When the Marquis de Lafayette visited the area in 1824, he was shown the unimpressive site, which was dedicated by the Army in 1826 to help guard the deep water port.

Fort Calhoun continued to sink, and many more boatloads of stone were dumped there over the next thirty-five years. By 1835 the Army had spent $1,380,333.68—almost as much as it had spent on Fort Monroe–and the island fort was still only one-third complete.

By the time of the Civil War, Fort Calhoun had fifty-two casemates, but it was still not ready to receive its guns or troops. Early in the war, it was manned by a Federal Naval Brigade with its very powerful experimental cannon, the Sawyer Gun. The gun fired on the Confederates on land and sea—at Sewell's Point and at the C.S.S. *Virginia* (the former *Merrimack*) during the famous "Battle of the Ironclads." But little damage was done to either target.

After that incident, the Army renamed the island Fort Wool in honor of Major General John Ellis Wool, a Mexican War hero who then commanded Federal forces in Virginia from his headquarters at Fort Monroe.

For a very brief time during the war, Fort Wool was used as a prison. The commanding general of Fort Monroe stopped that

use in 1862, saying, "The water is bad and the heat is intense, and no citizen should be sent there for a light cause and without pretty clear evidence of guilt."

All during the Civil War, the Army continued to build up Fort Wool, appropriating $200,000 in 1864. But after the war, further efforts were partially suspended.

From 1902 to 1906, the Army built five concrete artillery batteries on Fort Wool, and during World War I they were fully manned. Personnel stationed on the Rip Raps also tended the anti-submarine net that stretched to Fort Monroe.

Unused for 20 years until the outbreak of World War II, the fort was rearmed with anti-aircraft guns, and an anti-submarine net was again installed. British actor Alec Guinness, commander of a British vessel that entered Hampton Roads in 1944, ran his ship afoul of the net and an adjacent minefield—an incident he later recorded in his autobiography.

Fort Monroe and Fort Wool were necessary in the event of coastal naval attacks, but modern warfare made them obsolete. The property was decommissioned in 1967 and returned to Virginia. The island continues to settle—an inch at a time—and remains an unusual piece of military and presidential history.

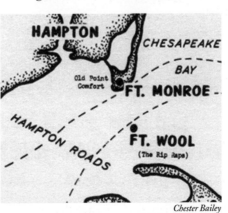

Chester Bailey

Forts Monroe and Wool

# 13 Battle of Big Bethel

IN THE AREA OF HAMPTON and York County known today as Bethel lies the site of the first pitched battle of the Civil War. In 1861, the area was a desolate countryside surrounding Big Bethel Church, which stood among a few small farms in rural Elizabeth City County, midway between Yorktown and Hampton.

Bethel Church went down in history as the site of the Confederacy's first victory. Amazingly, 1,400 newly inducted Confederates routed and drove from the battlefield 3,500 Union soldiers, costing the Confederates only one casualty. Some 200 Northern troops were either injured or killed.

*The Richmond Dispatch* declared: "It is one of the most extraordinary victories in the annals of war. Does not the hand of God seem manifest in this thing?" Big Bethel came six weeks before the well-documented blue and gray battle of Bull Run.

The battle took place June 10, 1861, two months after Virginia seceded. In that time, Virginia named Colonel John Bankhead Magruder, formerly of the U.S. Army, to command Peninsula forces against the Union threat coming from Fort Monroe. Commanding at Monroe at the outset was the colorful Major General Benjamin Butler, a peacetime lawyer who later aroused Southern hatred as "Beast" Butler for pillaging New Orleans.

Magruder's Confederate command post

*Casemate Museum Collection*
**Daniel Harvey Hill**

was at Yorktown. Several thousand Union troops were stationed at Monroe and Newport News. The Confederate leader at the battle was Colonel Daniel Harvey Hill, a North Carolinian serving under Magruder with his First Regiment of North Carolina Volunteers, a combat infantry unit.

He was the brother-in-law of General Thomas J. "Stonewall" Jackson and, in the early 1850s, taught math at Washington College in Lexington, Virginia, while Jackson taught at Virginia Military Institute a few blocks away. At the outbreak of the Civil War, Hill was serving as superintendent of the new North Carolina Military Institute in Charlotte, North Carolina, which he helped establish in 1859.

The daring, insolent Hill ventured with his troops from Yorktown on June 9, 1861, to attack Union soldiers at Bethel Church. There the Yankees had scrawled "death to the traitors" on church walls, and Hill wanted to punish them. Hill's contingent piled up defensive earthworks around the church. Then they waited inside them for Fort Monroe's troops to appear.

The Unionists did so on June 10—at least six regiments of them. Unfortunately for the untrained Union troops, two regiments mistook each other in the dark and fired on each other, killing two and wounding nineteen. Alarmed, the Union field commander called reinforcements to help invade Bethel Church's defenses.

Harper's Weekly Magazine, *June 29, 1861, Casemate Museum Collection*

Harper's Weekly Magazine, *June 29, 1861, Editor's Collection*

(*Top*) Colonel Abram Duryée's Zouaves (5th New York Volunteer Infantry) fought at Big Bethel
(*Above*) The Battle of Big Bethel took place on June 10, 1861

At one point during the firing, the Confederates sent five volunteers to burn a nearby house in which Hill thought the Yankees might be hiding. One Confederate soldier was killed in that foray, the only Southern death at Big Bethel.

After a while, the Union forces withdrew to Fortress Monroe. The Confederates claimed a victory, and news spread through the South. The *Charleston Courier* declared: "We learn that a great reaction has taken place among the money'd men in New York and Boston and that petitions are now circulating to be laid before Congress, asking the peaceful recognition of the Southern Confederacy."

The Peninsula remained ominously quiet until the following March and April, when the Union assembled invasion forces at Fort Monroe and Newport News at the beginning of General George B. McClellan's Peninsula Campaign of 1862.

During the tense first year after Virginia seceded, families from Hampton and adjoining counties fled to Richmond for safety. Some went first to Yorktown or Williamsburg, but when these two villages overflowed with people, many refugees went on to Richmond. Some Peninsula families rented quarters on Richmond's Church Hill and remained there until after Appomattox and the end of the conflict.

Hill, victor of the battle of Bethel, was promoted to brigadier general four weeks later and fought well on the Peninsula. Later, leading "D. H. Hill's Division" of Lee's Army of Northern Virginia, he participated in the battles at Seven Pines and Malvern Hill near Richmond and South Mountain and Antietam in Maryland. Weary of fame and a veteran of eleven pitched battles, Hill attempted to resign, but eventually accepted assignment to North Carolina as local commander and later joined the Army of Tennessee. But the caustic North

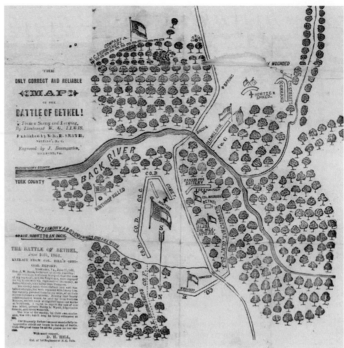

*Casemate Museum Collection*

**Big Bethel battlefield map**

Carolinian was removed from his command after Chickamauga because of his criticism of his superior, General Braxton Bragg.

Hill is remembered for his colorful language. In June 1863, he wrote to General John R. Cooke at Kinston, North Carolina, dispatching Cooke to another command. Affectionately, Hill added:

> It gives me real pain to part with you and your brave men. If I hated anything on earth, it is a Yankee, an exempt and a polecat. And next to the love of kindred, do I place my love for the brave soldiers in the ranks.

Hill went on to add, "May you have long life, great success in killing Yankees, a beautiful wife, and numerous progeny."

The last Confederate army to surrender was that of General Joseph E. Johnson on a field near Bentonville, North Carolina, and among those with him was a division commanded by Major General Hill.

Yes, Big Bethel in 1861 was an auspicious battle for the South and for Daniel Harvey Hill.

# 14 Balloons over Hampton

HOT-AIR BALLOON RIDES are popular tourist attractions across the nation today, but their predecessors were rising over Hampton and the nearby area as early as 1861, enabling Union commanders at Old Point to know what the Confederates were up to.

The first recorded use of balloons in the Civil War was at Fort Monroe in July 1861. The balloonist was John LaMountain of Troy, New York, who had accepted the job of aerial observer with Major General Benjamin Franklin Butler's command, based at Fort Monroe.

LaMountain had sought early in 1861 to entreat Union army officials to use balloons for reconnaissance work during wartime. Unfortunately, he had no influential backers, and his letter to Secretary of War Simon Cameron fell on deaf ears. He then turned directly to field commanders and contacted Butler, who asked him to come to eastern Virginia for a demonstration.

LaMountain brought his two balloons and other equipment to Old Point and made his first ascension on the evening of July 25. His balloon, like all others used during the Civil War, was called a "captive balloon" or

Frank Leslie's Illustrated Newspaper, *August 31, 1861, Casemate Museum Collection*
**Union balloon being tested at a camp near Fort Monroe**

*Casemate Museum Collection*

**John LaMountain**

"barrage balloon" and was secured by a rope to the ground to prevent its blowing into enemy territory.

Butler sent his young balloonist aloft for the first time over Monroe to learn the whereabouts of a Confederate force of two thousand men that had marched through York and Elizabeth City counties to round up slaves.

"When the Confederates arrived in Hampton on July 25," writes Richard Weinert Jr. in his history of Fort Monroe, "a large balloon suddenly rose from behind the Federal lines ... but a stiff wind was blowing at the time and [LaMountain] was unable to attain sufficient altitude for effective observation."

Several days later LaMountain tried again. He reached a height of 1,400 feet and had a good view over a radius of thirty miles, discovering an unknown Confederate camp near Sewell's Point on the Norfolk shore. A day later, LaMountain ascended again and was able to report that Confederate troops no longer occupied Hampton.

On August 3, 1861, Butler's balloonist tried a new trick. He attached his balloon rope to the Federal gunboat *Fanny*, which sailed out into Hampton Roads near the Confederate battery at Sewell's Point close to Norfolk. This time LaMountain ascended to two thousand feet to observe Confederate concentrations around the south shore of Hampton Roads. With LaMountain's balloon still aloft, the *Fanny* proceeded to sail toward Craney Island and Pig Point near the entrance to Norfolk.

Butler was disappointed with LaMountain, however, when he failed on August 6 to spot ten thousand Confederates who had marched east from Yorktown in an effort to lure Butler's troops out from Fort Monroe to fight.

It was during that foray that Colonel John B. Magruder gave the order to his soldiers to burn Hampton so its buildings could not be used by Butler to house slaves and Union troops. The little town of five hundred houses was nearly burned to the ground the next day. Most of the structures were ashes, with only a shell of St. John's Church and some isolated buildings standing.

The buildup of Confederates and the burning of Hampton created great concern in the Union headquarters at Fort Monroe.

LaMountain made his last ascensions for Butler on August 10, 1861, rising to 3,500 feet.

*Library of Congress*

**Thaddeus Lowe's balloon corps superseded LaMountain**

From that height, he discovered a large number of Magruder's Confederates fortifying the area around Young's Mill in neighboring Warwick County. That night Butler decided to join him on an ascent in the balloon from a base on board the Union tugboat *Adriatic* at Fort Monroe.

Butler was succeeded at Fort Monroe by Major General John Elias Wool, who dispatched the balloonist to army headquarters in Washington. There LaMountain was put to work as an observer for the Army of the Potomac, joining the already active work of Thaddeus Lowe, whose Union balloon corps had been organized earlier that year.

The Confederates also tried balloon observation during the Peninsula Campaign of 1862. The first Confederate ascension on April 13 was made by Lieutenant John Randolph Bryan, whose family owned Eagle Point plantation in Gloucester County. His balloon was an envelope made of cotton with a varnish coating and was a "montgolfiere"—or hot-air balloon.

After Bryan's flight over Yorktown was cut short by firing from Union troops nearby, Bryan tried to resign from the dangerous service. However, Confederate General Joseph E. Johnston, who had succeeded Magruder in defending the Peninsula, said no.

"Absolutely not," Johnston said. "You're the only experienced balloonist in the Confederate army."

On a second flight, Bryan's balloon drifted over Federal lines. In panic, Bryan destroyed his identification and his notes. When he landed safely in Confederate terrain, he was threatened with death as a spy until he convinced his captors that he was one of them.

*Casemate Museum Collection*

**Observation balloons were first used on the Virginia Peninsula**

# 15 Hampton Burns, August 1861

THE MOST FUTILE TRAGEDY in all Peninsula history was the burning of Hampton on August 7, 1861, by its own citizens. The flames destroyed nearly every building in the town of 2,500.

When Virginia voted earlier that year, on April 17, to secede from the Union, this area knew it was doomed to be one of the first battlegrounds of the Civil War. Sure enough, a huge Yankee army landed at Hampton in the next twelve months and then fought its way toward Richmond in an attempt to dislodge the Confederate government.

Tension was high in Confederate Hampton because of its proximity to the Union stronghold at Fort Monroe, the base of Union operations. That large moated sentinel never fell into Confederate hands, and was, from the beginning of the conflict, Yankee territory in the midst of Confederate homeland.

Why was Hampton burned?

The burning was carried out by men of the Old Dominion Dragoons, a cavalry unit made up of men from Elizabeth City County under the command of Captain Jefferson Phillips. They had no choice; they were following orders issued by Brigadier General John Bankhead Magruder,

"Prince John" to his friends.

Magruder, an Alabamian and graduate of West Point, had been sent to the Peninsula after Virginia seceded from the Union and following his resignation from the Union army. His Confederate assignment was to fortify the area surrounding Fort Monroe, commanded by Major General Benjamin Franklin Butler, and further up the Peninsula against an anticipated Federal move to capture Richmond.

Tension increased on May 23, 1861, when Butler refused to return three runaway Elizabeth City County slaves who had claimed sanctuary at Fort Monroe. When their owner attempted to reclaim them, Butler declared them "contraband of war" and declined. To show its strength, a Federal force from Monroe

Frank Leslie's Illustrated Newspaper, *June 8, 1861*, Daily Press *Archives*
**Runaway slaves fled to Fort Monroe seeking protection**

Frank Leslie's Illustrated Newspaper, *August 17, 1861, Casemate Museum Collection*

**Confederate soldiers run from house to house setting Hampton on fire**

marched that same day into Hampton and halted at the intersection of King and Queen streets, the town's center.

Wrote Major John B. Cary, ex-headmaster of Hampton Academy and a Confederate officer, the act "seemed at first to wear a very ugly aspect from which, happily, resulted in no damage save the alarm of our women and children and the excitement of our citizens."

Hastily, Cary and Colonel Northcott Phelps of Fort Monroe met and agreed to keep the peace. Accordingly, the Union troops left Hampton unmolested and marched back to Monroe.

Soon, however, an outflow of slaves from farms in the Hampton Roads area converged on Fort Monroe seeking emancipation and encamped in the area between Hampton and Monroe, part of which was the town of Chesapeake City, later renamed Phoebus.

By early August, the buildup of runaways at Monroe forced Butler to move them into a "slab town" of makeshift houses along Mill Creek. Magruder read of this decision in a dispatch published in the *New York Tribune* and decided to burn Hampton and avert a takeover by Unionists. Magruder acted to show the Confederacy's defiance.

Many believed his decision was a vain and foolhardy move. Other Virginia towns survived Union occupation, but Hampton suffered major losses for a second time. The city had been pillaged by the British in 1813, but had recovered by 1861.

Hampton's Confederates took pride in setting fire to their own homes to show their sacrifice. Some five hundred structures were destroyed, and St. John's Church was gutted. William West, whose father, Parker West,

Frank Leslie's Illustrated Newspaper, *August 10, 1861, Hampton History Museum*

Harper's Weekly Magazine, *August 31, 1861, Casemate Museum Collection*

(*Top*) Hampton burning, as viewed from a mansion rooftop across the water
(*Above*) Nearly five hundred structures were destroyed in the 1861 fire

owned a fine Hampton town house, put it to the torch.

Today at the Hampton History Museum, an interesting document gives Lieutenant Phillips's account of the fire. It reads in part:

> He [Magruder] handed me a Northern paper and, pointing to an item which said the Federal forces contemplated occupying Hampton as winter quarters, said he had concluded to burn Hampton; ordered me to take four companies—two cavalry and two infantry—to proceed to Hampton and burn it. ...
>
> Accordingly, shortly after dark we took up line of march for the town crossing New Market bridge, which had been destroyed but partially repaired for this occasion, moved straight down the country road, stopping on the west wall of old St. John's churchyard. ...
>
> I placed them [a company of twenty men] at the foot of Hampton bridge, telling them that if they were fired upon, they would be supported. [I then gave] orders that each company should fire one quarter of the town, divided at the cross streets. ... Flames were seen bursting from the buildings on all sides, till it appeared the town was a mass of flames.

Then, Phillips led his troops up the Sawyer Swamp Road to Magruder's headquarters and reported the mission accomplished.

No lives were lost in the sad disaster, but many families lost all their property and belongings. Some even had to seek refuge at Fort Monroe. Others escaped to Williamsburg and Richmond. Federal troops later moved to occupy the ruins of Hampton.

A war correspondent who observed the fire reported in *The Philadelphia Inquirer*:

> A more desolate sight cannot be imagined than is Hampton today. Last evening it was one of the most beautiful villages on the continent, with a wealth of cottages and villas, embowered in luxurious foliage and adorned with taste. ... Only some half-dozen small houses are left.

Elizabeth City County's burned courthouse was not rebuilt until 1876, and the gutted interior of St. John's was eventually restored. After the Civil War, the town was slowly rebuilt.

Regarding the burning of Hampton, Union Major General Butler wrote: "I confess myself so poor a soldier as not to be able to see the strategical importance of this movement."

**Lone man stands amid ruins in Hampton**

# 16 Lincoln Visits Fort Monroe

**P**RESIDENT LINCOLN paid an important visit to Fort Monroe in the winter of 1865, when he met secretly with three major officials of the Confederate States of America in an effort to end the war.

It's a shame that effort failed, for Lincoln was willing to recommend to Congress that Southern slave-owners be paid for their slaves by the United States if the South would return to the Union. It didn't work. As we know, Confederate General Robert E. Lee fought on to defeat on April 9, 1865, just two months after the peace conference. The South thereby lost its hope for independence and its slaves, too.

The Hampton Roads Peace Conference took place February 3, 1865, in the salon of the *River Queen*, a side-wheeler steamboat, "under the guns of Fort Monroe." Accompanying the president down the river from Washington was Secretary of State William H. Seward. They met with three Confederates from Richmond: Confederate Vice President Alexander H. Stephens of Georgia, Assistant Secretary of War and former Alamama Supreme Court Justice John A. Campbell, and former Virginia Senator Robert M. T. Hunter.

After having been assured by Army General-in-Chief Ulysses S. Grant that the intentions of the Confederate "peace" commissioners were good, Lincoln departed from Annapolis on the steamer *Thomas Collyer*. He arrived at Fortress Monroe about 10 p.m. February 2. Earlier that day, the Confederate leaders had traveled down the James River from Petersburg on the steamship *Mary Martin*.

According to presidential historian Doris Kearns Goodwin, in her volume *Team of Rivals—The Political Genius of Abraham Lincoln*,

the four-hour meeting began the next day "in the salon of the *River Queen* [Grant's flagship], which had been lashed to the *Mary Martin* the night before and 'gaily decked out with a super-abundance of streamers and flags.'"

It was an awkward reunion for Lincoln and Stephens, for they had been friends and fellow congressmen before the war.

Stephens was a small, wiry man weighing less than ninety pounds. Like Lee and many other Southerners, he had opposed secession, but when the war came, he accepted the vice presidency of the Confederacy. He arrived on the *River Queen* in a huge overcoat, muffler,

Lincoln, An Illustrated Biography, *1992*

**Lincoln meets with Confederate officials**

**The Hampton Roads Peace Conference was held aboard the *River Queen***

and several shawls to fight off the winter weather and the winds off the water. Lincoln broke the tension with humor, as he often did. "Never have I seen so small a nubbin come out of so much husk," he said to the tiny Stephens, who related the incident later in a newspaper interview.

Nothing came of the meeting except Lincoln's release from a Northern military prison of Stephens's nephew, who had been taken prisoner in battle. With the peace, the war ground bloodily on, and Grant's siege of Richmond and Petersburg ultimately forced Lee's surrender at Appomattox on April 9.

Lincoln had a big hand in his army's conduct of the war, and he often sailed down the Potomac to Virginia in the four years of fighting. In addition to his two visits to Monroe, he also visited City Point (now Hopewell) and Berkeley on the James, where he discussed the war with General George B. McClellan. He came to Richmond,

Lincoln, An Illustrated Biography, *1992*
**Alexander H. Stephens**

the ex-Confederate capital, shortly after the siege ended.

His earlier visit to Fort Monroe came in May 1862, a year after the war started. He was impatient at McClellan's delay in pushing up the Peninsula to Richmond. The president, accompanied by Secretary of War Edwin M. Stanton, Secretary of the Treasury Salmon P. Chase, and Brigadier General Egbert L. Viele, came by the treasury cutter *Miami* to Fort Monroe, ending the twenty-seven hour trip the evening of May 6, the day after McClellan captured Williamsburg.

Ironically, Lincoln visited Monroe not to chastise McClellan, but at the request of General John Ellis Wool, commander of the fort. He wanted the president on hand for the anticipated attack on Confederate defenses in Norfolk.

The president stayed at the commanding officer's quarters at Monroe. He also participated in what historians have called "a council of war" as plans were discussed regarding Norfolk.

Federal forces on Fort Wool—the Rip Raps—shelled Confederates across the water at Sewell's Point, but the Confederates stood firm. A closer naval bombardment by ship also failed to dislodge the gray line.

According to accounts, Lincoln was not happy with the failure to silence the Confederate fortifications at Sewell's Point and decided to make a personal reconnaissance of the scene, later determining that a landing of Federal troops near what is now Ocean View would be better.

The landing was accomplished by about six thousand troops on May 9, and, by May 11, the Union army entered Norfolk, which had surrendered. Lincoln watched some of the action from Fort Wool. Additionally, the Confederates scuttled their ironclad *Merrimack*, ending the two-month Hampton Roads stalemate with the Union's *Monitor*.

Daily Press *Archives*
**George B. McClellan**

The house that sheltered Lincoln at Monroe, known as Quarters 1, is still in use there. It was built in the neat Southern form of other officers' quarters, including the house wherein Lieutenant and Mrs. Robert E. Lee had lived with their family in the 1830s. Both are built in a style that suggests nineteenth-century Mississippi cotton mansions, appropriately framed by old live oaks, which give the casemate area of Monroe such an old-time Southern flavor.

Quite naturally, Fort Monroe played host to numerous important military officials through the years, as well as other presidents —Andrew Jackson, John Tyler, Millard Fillmore, James A. Garfield, Rutherford B. Hayes, Theodore Roosevelt, Woodrow Wilson, Franklin D. Roosevelt, and Harry S. Truman. Today, it continues to serve as the nation's third-oldest active military fortification—but after 2011, when the military leaves, there will be more history. But that's another story.

*Casemate Museum Collection*
**Lincoln stayed at Quarters 1 during his 1861 visit**

# 17 James S. Darling, "65er"

VIRGINIANS OFTEN make a distinction between "come-heres" and "stay-puts"—those who move to town and those who've been around since Adam. That is especially true in an old town like Hampton, which has been in business ever since the first English settlers in 1609 dropped a couple of their number at Old Point to keep watch for Spanish invaders.

Partially burned in 1813 and nearly destroyed in the Civil War, Hampton has rebuilt each time. In its revival after 1865, it attracted as residents a lot of Yankees who had been Union soldiers or Freedmen's Bureau officials in the "Late Unpleasantness." They liked Virginia and chose to stay.

*Hampton History Museum*
**James S. Darling**

Early twentieth-century Hamptonians called them "carpetbaggers" and "65ers," but they included some of the best citizens Hampton ever had. An important one was Samuel Chapman Armstrong, who founded Hampton Institute. Another was James Sands Darling, who brought his wife and year-old son here in 1866 on a schooner loaded with lumber to rebuild Hampton's houses burned in the Civil War.

"Old J. S.," as he was called, died back in 1900 at the age of 68, but the family's legacy is well remembered. His son Frank W. Darling died in 1941, and his grandson, "Young J. S.," died at 52 in 1951.

What was impressive about the Darlings was their Yankee enterprise and generosity—especially their generosity. There are countless stories of their help to Hampton Institute, St. John's Church, and aspiring students. Their civic spirit was wonderful to behold. They were loved by black and white.

Old J. S. was born in New York City in 1832, the son of an English-born ship joiner. He grew up in the present midtown New York, now covered with skyscrapers. When he was 11, his mother died, and he was hired out to an aunt to work on her Long Island farm. From there, he went to his brother's Long Island shipway to learn a trade and became a partner.

The Darling brothers did pretty well until the Civil War came along. Discouraged in New York, 33-year-old James Darling sailed to Virginia after Appomattox to find a new career. He chose the burned-over village of Hampton. He installed his family in a house on King Street close to his mill and brought a shipload of lumber down to build other houses. Soon he bought a sawmill and gristmill on King Street near his house.

After Hampton grew west in the 1880s, J. S. built a new house on the present Victoria Boulevard, near Armistead Avenue.

Darling liked Southerners and had sympathized with them in the Civil War. He paid a

Darling's oyster plant dominated downtown Hampton for years

"Hessian" to fight for him.

As Darling prospered in Hampton, he extended his reach. In 1879, he formed a partnership with William Smithers and built a fish oil factory on the Eastern Shore. Unfortunately, a hurricane soon destroyed it, and the partners lost their shirts.

Undiscouraged, 50-year-old Darling turned to tonging oysters in Hampton Roads. And there, as his grandson Frank Cumming told the story, he was spotted by his old friend William Ballard, a prosperous Norfolk oyster buyer. Ballard lent him money to rebuild. The revived fish oil factory was long operated on Back River near Grand View.

Darling went broke again when his lumber mill failed. However, his chief employee, Bill Sparks, an African American mill-hand, refused to be turned off. "Boss, you can just feed me," he told Darling. The mill was restarted, and it prospered. Darling paid his faithful helper, and in his will left him a farm on the Eastern Shore.

In 1881, Darling and his son formed J. S. Darling and Son, Oyster Planters and Packers, which became the largest business of it kind inthe world. It closed in 1979.

In 1882, when Hampton bar was opened by the state for oyster-planting, J. S. rented acreage and began oystering. Hampton oysters proved highly salable, and J. S. had to hire hundreds of oyster shuckers. The mountains of oyster shells at his plant on Hampton River were a landmark long after his death. There were other measures of his success.

In 1888, J. S. took another flyer and built a street railway with the Schmelz brothers to connect Hampton and Old Point Comfort. It flourished, and, three years later, they extended it down the new Victoria Avenue to Newport News. The trolley provided quick and cheap transport between the two cities. It also did much to build up Collis Huntington's shipyard, which he had opened at Newport News in 1886.

Many yard employees found it easy to work in Newport News and live in Hampton. Wrote the *Phoebus Sentinel* of Darling's railway in 1900:

> Its effect on the growth and prosperity of Hampton was marked from the day the first car passed over it. Hundreds of people came to live in the West End of Hampton near the line. The cars quickly became crowded, and the electric railway recognized as a successful venture.

Many Peninsula residents took Sunday

outings to Old Point over the trolleys. Mrs. Frederick Hartel of Williamsburg, whose father was then an army officer at Fort Monroe, recalls stylish ladies and gentlemen stepping off the street car near the Old Chamberlin Hotel to enjoy dining and dancing and Sunday band concerts. That was the age of Victor Herbert, Sousa, and "The Blue Danube."

After he built the trolley line to Buckroe, J. S. teamed with son Frank to create what the *Phoebus Sentinel* described as "a magnificent hotel" at Buckroe Beach plus a dance and picnic pavilion. To his wife, who was visiting relatives in the North, young Frank Darling, in the early 1900s, wrote proudly of the first day's "good profit" of "several dollars." Unfortunately, though, the Buckroe trolley that same day struck a cow.

J. S. and the Schmelzes sold the trolley line two years before he died, bringing him a profit of $16,000—more than he expected. He gave a party for his trolley employees on Christmas Day in 1898 and divided the sum among them in checks ranging from $50 to $1,000. The old man wept as he thanked his men, and they wept in gratitude for the gift.

"No one was overlooked." reported the *Sentinel*, "from the man who greased the tracks on up. It was a splendid Christmas gift."

The J. S. Darlings had three children, two of whom lived to maturity. Daughter Grace married James Cumming and had seven children. The Darlings' son, Frank, married Mary "Mollie" Gorton, who taught Indian students at Hampton Institute. Their only child, J. S. Darling II, grew up at Cedar Hall, which the Darlings had built on Hampton River early in the 1900s. It was razed years ago and is now a waterside residential area.

Frank Darling's wife, Mollie, outlived both her husband and her son, dying in 1957 at Cedar Hall. She loved music, books, theatricals—anything creative. "Cedar Hall when the Darlings lived there was full of laughter," says a Hamptonian. Mollie organized the Cedar Hall Reading Club, several theatrical groups and taught Sunday school at St. John's for forty years. The family gave the St. John's window, contributed marble steps for the parish house, and other gifts. "The Darlings were forever doing things for people," a friend recalled.

J. S. Darling II inherited his parents' business and civic interests. He created and served as chairman until his death of the Hampton Roads Sanitation Commission. His three children are Mrs. James Tormey, the former Ann Darling of Hampton, Sally Darling, an actress and off-Broadway producer of New York, and J. S. "Jock" Darling III, longtime organist at Bruton Parish Church and harpsichordist of Williamsburg.

Yankees or not, the Darlings became part of the Peninsula mainstream at the end of the Civil War and remained so for years and years. Old J. S. may have been a "carpetbagger," but he soon became a rare and valuable citizen—one of the key figures in Hampton's revival. Many legacies of the Darlings

*Hampton History Museum*

**Darling built Hampton–Old Point trolley line**

and the Cummings live on in Hampton, including Darling Memorial Stadium. Frank Darling gave the land for the stadium in memory of his father.

The moral of all this seems to be that newcomers have brought to the Peninsula many blessings. Yankees they were, but Hamptonians have frequently said "Thank God" for the Armstrongs, the Cummings, the Darlings, and the rest of the "come-heres." Hampton wouldn't be the same without them.

# 18 The Rise of a German Baker

THE RISE OF THE Peninsula from the ruins of the Civil War is an epic, taken too much for granted today. Seldom in history has a defeated people been so desolated as Virginians were after Appomattox.

Yet this area made a comeback. From the cinders of Hampton, a great community developed. The men who created a trolley system, waterworks, banks, stores, and businesses galore should get just as much credit as the arrival of the railroad, the shipyard, and the military.

It was a revolution for a section of the world that had stuck largely to farming and fishing since Jamestown's time. Many people hated the change. Ellen Glasgow, who wrote novels in Richmond in the early twentieth century, said she missed the courtly manners of the plantation age. She did not like industry. But geography dictated that Hampton after 1865 would be part of a center of defense and a rebuilt seafood industry.

One man who anticipated that was Francis Anton Schmelz, a German who had emigrated to the United States before the Civil War. After serving in the Confederacy, he mustered out at Hampton in 1865 and started a bakery and confectionery on Queen Street. He did so well he sent his two sons to college.

Stories still circulate about the Schmelzes' enterprise. One was that they sent a load of pastries by trolley each workday from Hampton to the Newport News shipyard to be sold outside the gates for snacks and lunch. Another was that Francis Schmelz got his start crabbing with a hand line on the Hampton waterfront. With a piece of meat as bait, he was said to have caught enough crabs to get a start.

Virginia had few banks in the Schmelzes' days. Until then, merchants performed services now handled by banks. The first Peninsula banks were the First National and the Citizens and Marine, both begun in Newport News in 1889.

The Schmelz brothers were George Anton and Henry, sons of Francis Schmelz. They had prospered in their father's bakery and decided to open a small privately owned bank in the rear of Henry's King Street bakery.

The 1880s were a time of Peninsula growth. Bank credit was needed to buy real estate, build stores and houses, and open businesses. The Schmelz brothers provided it.

The Schmelzes' "back room bank" flourished. A 1911 newspaper says it "was so successful and the natural ability of the two brothers was so apparent that they decided to enter the banking business in all its branches." They opened their first full bank at King and Queen streets. Success enabled them in 1902 to buy out the rival Bank of Hampton and consolidate under that name.

In 1890, the brothers started another bank in Newport News at 25th Street and Washing-

*Hampton History Museum*

**George Anton Schmelz**

ton Avenue. It, too, was originally a private bank, whose stock was held by the two brothers alone. It went public in 1912. By that time, it had become the largest private bank in the South.

In 1931, long after the two brothers' deaths, Schmelz Brothers' Bank sold its assets to the First National Bank of Newport News. The Schmelz brothers had not been able to reopen its doors after the Roosevelt bank moratorium of 1931, but its assets were found fully adequate to pay off depositors. Nobody lost a cent!

They married sisters, Mattie and Georgia Hickman. Their own sisters married Howard Collier and Robert Hudgins, both of Hampton. George and his wife reared five daughters, and Henry and his wife had two daughters.

**SCHMELZ BROS., BANKERS,**
NEWPORT NEWS. VA.
**DO A GENERAL BANKING BUSINESS.**
Accounts of individuals, firms and corporations solicited.
Collections made on all parts of the country. Foreign exchanges bought and sold at lowest rates. Foreign drafts issued on all parts of the world.
**IN OUR DIME SAVINGS DEPARTMENT**
Deposits received from 10 cents to $5,000.00 and interest allowed at the rate of 4 PER CENT. PER ANNUM.
**SAFETY DEPOSIT BOXES FOR RENT.**
Only safety boxes in the city secured by time locks.

*Daily Press Archives*

An 1898 advertisement for Schmelz Brothers Bank

The Schmelz boys also started other enterprises. With Frank W. Darling of Hampton, they built the Newport News and Old Point Railway and Electric Company. Its purpose was to provide fast and cheap transport for workers at the shipyard. Trolleys first rolled in Hampton and then spread to Newport News and westward into Warwick County. The company later became the Citizens Rapid Transit, which ultimately became Pen Tran and is now a part of Hampton Roads Transit.

The now prosperous George Schmelz was also the chief stockholder in an infant Newport News paper that later merged to become the morning *Daily Press* and the afternoon *Times-Herald* papers, and now the merged *Daily Press*. He was chief mover in the Hampton, Phoebus, and Fort Monroe Gas Corporation and an officer of McMenamin Crab Picking House, then a big plant on Hampton River. It helped Hampton to become Virginia's "Crab Town."

In that age of local banks, George Schmelz served on the boards of two in Richmond and Hampton and one in Newport News. His office, where he jovially met all comers, was a corner of the Schmelz bank in Newport News. He came to work by trolley, like most other people then.

The brothers always lived in Hampton.

Like many men then, George Schmelz taught a Sunday school class before morning service at Hampton's Memorial Baptist Church. His wife had given funds to build the church. Inspired by her example, Schmelz organized its men's class, which was "said to be the largest in Virginia, if not in the South," according to an early *Daily Press*.

Hampton was shocked in 1909 when Mrs. George Schmelz died at 50, leaving her five young daughters. The community was equally stricken in 1911 when George himself died at Johns Hopkins Hospital in Baltimore at 57. Tributes poured in. "He was easily the most promising figure in the Peninsula business world," wrote an editorialist.

A newspaper account of Schmelz's funeral gives insight into life in 1911. When the casket reached Richmond from Baltimore on its way to Hampton, it was met by an honor guard of friends, who accompanied it on the train the rest of the way. Delegations of mourners waited at C&O depots in Newport News and in Hampton.

At Hampton, Henry Lane Schmelz, almost crushed by his brother's death, received the condolences of his intimate friends as he made his way to his carriage. At the service, President Frederic W. Boatwright of Richmond College led a long procession of pallbearers. They included Frank W. Darling, Henry C. Blackiston, Nelson Groome, Hunter Booker, Albert Howe, and Jacob Heffelfinger of Hampton; Douglas Smith and Robert P. Holt of Newport News; Simon R. Curtis of Lee Hall; and John M. Miller, a Richmond banker.

Three years after George died, his brother, Henry, followed at 61. He had been ill in bed for eight months. Wrote the *Daily Press*, "There is little question but what Mr. Schmelz was the best all around banking man in Eastern Virginia." He was a director of banks in Hampton, Newport News, Phoebus, Norfolk, and Richmond.

No descendants bearing the name Schmelz are on the Peninsula today, but the family survived under other names. One member was William R. Van Buren Jr., former president and treasurer and part owner of the *Daily Press*, grandson of George Schmelz. Other descendants bear the names Collier, Hudgins, Phillips, Robinson, Coenen, and Lasch, though not all are in the area.

Hampton's first three Schmelzes—immigrant Francis and sons Henry and George—played a notable part in the rise of the city. They rubbed elbows with other empire builders: Harrison Phoebus of Old Point, Frank Darling of Hampton, and Collis Huntington of Newport News. It was such men as these who moved Hampton and the area forward quickly and businesslike.

Newport News: 325 Years

**Schmelz Brothers Bank building in Newport News**

# 19 General Armstrong's School

IN HAWAII, if you look carefully at various historical institutions, you may come across the footprints of a Hampton figure admired by many persons. He was Samuel Chapman Armstrong, a Hawaii-bred teacher who rose to be a general in the Civil War and spent the rest of his life teaching African Americans to become citizens.

He was the founder of Hampton Normal and Agricultural Institute, now Hampton University.

In a historic house of an 1830s Congregationalist missionary (the Lyman Mission House) in downtown Hilo, the story of the Reverend Richard B. Armstrong is told. He had come to Hawaii in a great American missionary outpouring of the early 1800s. Like many fellow Congregationalists from New England's colleges, he spent his life Christianizing the amiable Polynesians of the Sandwich Islands— today known as the Hawaiian chain.

The face of Richard Armstrong was gentle yet strong. Looking at his picture in the Lyman House Museum, one could understand how he was chosen to be commissioner of education for the islands. Though Hawaiians before Congregationalism had lived a good life of dancing and laughter, they lacked an alphabet and nearly everything else that Western ingenuity had devised since the Middle Ages. Along with Christianity, Armstrong and his Congregationalists brought to Hawaii reading, writing, arithmetic, and medicine.

Armstrong's sixth child was Samuel Chapman, born on Maui in 1839 and sent back to Williams College in Williamstown, Massachusetts, in 1858 to be educated under the great Mark Hopkins. In addition to his father's good looks, he inherited a missionary impulse. He grew up wanting to help people, to spread the New England mixture of puritanism and materialism that had made those psalm-singing Northerners so rich and influential.

Samuel Armstrong set out to be a teacher, but the Civil War broke out while he was in college and he joined the Union Army. He was assigned to units of blacks, eventually becoming colonel in command of the 8th and 9th U.S. Colored Troops. That experience convinced him "of the excellent qualities and capacities of the freedman. Their quick response to good treatment and to discipline was a constant surprise," Armstrong wrote.

He was captured by Confederates at Harper's Ferry in 1862 but, after an exchange of prisoners, returned to duty and fought until the war's end.

After Appomattox, he was sent to Old Point by the Freedmen's Bureau to help the

Daily Press *Archives*
**Samuel Chapman Armstrong**

Virginia Hall, designed by Richard Morris Hunt, was built in 1874

Teacher lectures in Hampton's Assembly Room

he heard a call he thought came from God. It was to start a school for African Americans like the Hilo Training School for Native Hawaiians that his father had created in Hawaii.

By this time a brigadier, young Samuel begged money from the American Missionary Society to buy Little Scotland, a farm on Hampton River. Congregationalist church members and the institution itself proved generous donors, and acreage was bought as the site for the school. The former plantation house, now called Mansion House, remains the residence of the university president. The society first asked an older man to run the school. When he declined, they turned to Armstrong.

The Institute that began in 1868 had about twenty-five students, taught by whites. In many ways, it resembled Howard, a school for African Americans founded in the District of Columbia a year earlier by another Freedmen's Bureau general, O. O. Howard. Each has grown into a national

thousands of blacks who had been emancipated and were encamped around Fort Monroe without homes or jobs. Armstrong had begun teaching them to read and write, when suddenly

institution with students from many states and lands. Armstrong and Howard were pioneers.

Armstrong enlisted old friends to help start his school, including U.S. Senator (later President) James Garfield and Williams College President Mark Hopkins. Another supporter was Quaker poet John Greenleaf Whittier. From the beginning, many wealthy and influential Northern industrialists also served on Hampton's board, including John D. Rockefeller Sr. and later his son John D. Rockefeller Jr.

Reflecting on his family's educational work, the young Armstrong wrote that his father's experience in "the emancipation, enfranchisement and Christian civilization of a dark-skinned Polynesian people in many respects like the Negro race" suggested his plans for Hampton.

The Institute was not popular with Virginians for a long time. The war was too recent, and Northerners (they were called "Yankees") were regarded dubiously. The campus was a little world to itself. In 1870, the Institute was incorporated by the state.

The Armstrongs and other white teachers were snubbed by locals, but the school grew. By 1874, it had $37,000, much of it raised by the student choir in concerts through the North, singing spirituals and gospel songs.

"I have been in the traveling show business the last two years," Armstrong wrote a friend. "Have given over 300 concerts with the Hampton students (many ex-slaves). This is a rough and terrible fight with difficulties, but I think I'm on top."

In those early years, Armstrong often wrote to influential and wealthy men to obtain support for his school. In one statement, he declared:

> The thing to be done was clear. To train selected Negro youth who should go out and teach and lead their people, first by example, by getting land and homes; to give them not a dollar that they could earn for themselves; to teach respect for labor, to replace stupid drudgery with skilled hands; and to build up an industrial system, for the sake not only of self-support and industrial labor, but also for the sake of character.
>
> And it seems equally clear that the people of the country would support a wise word for the freedman.

**The campus of Hampton Normal and Agricultural Institute in 1892**

Tower of Memorial Chapel dominates this view of Hampton University

A formal education program for Indians was established at Hampton Institute in 1878 with some financial support from the federal government (*see* Chapter 20). This began the Institute's lasting commitment to serving a multicultural population.

The educator was considered by many whites to be a troublemaker. Liberal blacks called him a white racist. Still, Armstrong had faith and carried on. He believed that black people could only assume responsibility as citizens if they were educated and able to support themselves.

"I tell you," he wrote in the 1880s,

the present is the grandest time the world ever saw. The African race is before the world, and all mankind is looking to see whether the African will show himself equal to the opportunity. And what is this opportunity? It is to demonstrate that he is a man—that he has the highest elements of manhood, courage, perseverance and honor. That he is not only worthy of freedom but able to win it.

One of the Institute's early students was Booker T. Washington, who went there from a Rocky Mount, Virginia, farm and later was principal of Tuskegee Institute in Alabama. Teachers were trained as well as nurses, artisans,

**Booker T. Washington**

and homemakers. Many became preachers, for Southern blacks were and remained church-oriented.

When Armstrong's young wife, Emma Dean Walker, of Stockbridge, Massachusetts, died in 1878, she left him two daughters, aged 6 and 8, to raise. He did so and waited a decade before marrying again. His second wife was Mary Alice Ford of Lisbon, New Hampshire, who for a number of years had been a teacher at the Institute.

On a trip north in 1892, he became paralyzed, but his friend Collis Huntington sent his private rail car to bring Armstrong back to Hampton. The two had become friends when Huntington came to Newport News in 1880 to create a port for his C&O railway, and they worked together on schooling and jobs for African Americans.

Armstrong died in 1893, only a few months after he had walked out to the Institute shoreline to watch a great fleet of American naval vessels return from its global voyage from Hampton Roads to celebrate the 400th anniversary of Columbus's arrival in the New World.

Armstrong was buried on the campus with a stone from Hawaii at his head. But the best memorial was the Institute he founded.

His widow, who went north with her children after his death, lived until 1958. Armstrong's son-in-law Arthur Howe was president of Hampton Institute from 1930 to 1940, and, in 1949, Alonzo Graseano Moron was chosen its first African American president. The current Hampton University president is Dr. William R. Harvey, who has led the school since 1978.

The Armstrong name remained in Hampton as long as his nephew, Richard Armstrong, and his brothers, Kalani and Matt, lived on Armstrong Point, not far from the Institute. After their deaths, the area retook its earlier name: Ivy Home Farms.

But Samuel Armstrong will never be forgotten. Hampton University is today a prestigious and well-endowed liberal arts institution known around the world. Like his missionary father in Hawaii, Armstrong left his world better than he had found it.

*Hampton University Archives*

**Indian students first came to Hampton Institute in 1878**

# 20 Emancipation in Education

THIS PENINSULA has a relatively high percentage of African American citizens, due, in part, to the Emancipation Proclamation issued by President Abraham Lincoln in the midst of the Civil War. When he declared all slaves in federally held territory to be free after January 1, 1863, great numbers of black people in Tidewater left their masters' farms to claim freedom at Fort Monroe.

Countless African American families later built shanties in what is now Phoebus and other nearby areas, living in them until after Reconstruction days. Many of their descendants decided to remain on the Peninsula and have become active in civic and community groups.

With Lincoln's proclamation, two organizations soon moved in to help the African Americans who sought the protection of Federal forces. One was the American Missionary Society, an organization established by North-

ern Congregationalists, which sent teachers to set up schools for blacks and conduct worship services. The other was the federal government's Freedom Bureau.

Soon the burned-out Elizabeth City Courthouse was reclaimed as a school for five hundred African Americans.

The Reverend Lewis Lockwood was the first missionary to arrive and to teach. A mission worker named C. P. Day ran the Courthouse School, dividing students into primary and higher departments. Black and white volunteers taught African Americans of all ages, for few slaves of any age could read or write.

Major General Benjamin Butler constructed a wooden school building for the former slaves in 1863 near what would be called Emancipation Oak, on the present Hampton University campus. It was named Butler School and its funds came from the federal govern-

Harper's Weekly Magazine, *May 1861, Hampton History Museum*

**Slaves raced over bridge to "Freedom's Fort" to secure their freedom**

"Slabtown" developed on the edge of Hampton's burned ruins

ment. The site was appropriate because in 1861 Mrs. Mary Smith Peake taught young slaves reading and writing under that oak tree.

Because of the overcrowding, another large school was built in Hampton at "Slabtown" on the road to Buckroe Beach. Butler School ultimately became a free public school about 1871.

Following the war, the Freedmen's Bureau appointed Samuel Armstrong as its representative in Hampton. He immediately saw the need for schools to teach African Americans not only how to read and write but also how to make a living as farmers, teachers, nurses, mechanics, and so on. With the help of friends and his Congregational church, Armstrong founded the Hampton Normal and Agricultural Institute in 1868.

To be admitted to Hampton Institute, a student had to be between 15 and 25 and be able to read at the fifth-grade level.

Fortunately, the school soon received an unexpected windfall from the federal government. It was chosen, along with the newly founded and similarly vocational Virginia Polytechnic Institute, to divide Virginia's share of federal funds granted under the Morrill Land Grant Act.

Another interesting, but very important element in the development of Hampton began in 1878 with the admission to the school of seventeen Indians—Native Americans—who, like the African Americans, had very few educational opportunities across the country. These children were "prisoners" from the Indian Wars.

A correspondent writing in *Harper's New Monthly Magazine* in 1881 recalled that a young Army captain, R. H. Pratt, who had been dealing with Indian prisoners in Florida for several years, finally arranged for them to either be returned to their lands or to go to school. Hampton Institute then agreed to take them in 1778.

> It was not, therefore, in utter dismay that the [students] of Hampton were roused from their slumbers one April night by a steamboat's war-whoop, heralding the mid-night raid of sixty ex-warriors upon their peaceful shores, and hastened out to meet the invaders with hot coffee instead of rifle-balls, to welcome some of them as new students and bid the rest godspeed to their homes in Indian Territory.

**Butler School was founded in 1863 for freedmen**

like their African American schoolmates, were required to learn to write as well as study math. The coeducation of the sexes "is regarded at Hampton as essential in the development of both these races in which woman has been so long degraded," *Harper's Magazine* said.

Colita Nichols Fairfax, in her book *Hampton, Virginia*, wrote, "despite student health problems and paternalistic attitudes of the Indian Bureau about co-mingling the two disadvantaged populations, Armstrong assured them that the school's mission had not been hampered."

After several years, a dozen or so Indian chiefs came to Hampton to see the children of their tribes. They examined every aspect of the school. During a schoolwide meeting, attended by the chiefs, one Indian girl stood up and "told her people's rulers what the school was to her, and begged them to send all the children to learn the good road." The chiefs listened "with respectful attention," the magazine article reported.

The Indian School remained active through the 1892 school year, after which the federal government withdrew its financial support. Some Indians continued to come, and Fairfax noted that more than 1,300 Indians from sixty-five tribes had been educated at Hampton Institute by 1923.

Armstrong headed Hampton until he died in 1893. By that time, the vocational school had an enrollment of 638 African American and 188 Indian students plus 300 African American youngsters in its children's primary school. The campus boasted about fifty buildings.

Six months later, Hampton received another group of Indians, "forty-nine young Dakotas, chiefly Sioux, with a few Mandans, Rees, and Gros Ventres, for each of whom the United States stood pledged to appropriate $167, reduced subsequently to $150 yearly, while it should keep them at school."

Pratt saw immediately that his ideas were working at Hampton, thanks to Armstrong, so he began efforts to build an Indian School, based upon Armstrong's Hampton pattern. By the fall of 1879, Carlisle Barracks, a former army post, had been selected, and Carlisle Indian School was born.

Regarding Hampton's efforts, *Harper's Magazine* said,

> The hospitality of the colored students, somewhat overtaxed by the inroad of nearly double the number of boys expected, before their new quarters were ready for them, revived with the changes wrought by soap and water, and won full victory when, on taking possession of their new "wigwam" a month later, the Dakotas made a spontaneous petition, through their interpreter, for colored room-mates for "help talk English."

In addition to learning English, the Indians,

# 21 National Soldiers' Home

NESTLED ON THE PHOEBUS shore near the entrance to Hampton River is a massive, handsome brick building that looks across Hampton Roads toward Norfolk. Officially, it is the Hampton Veterans Affairs Medical Center, but most people just call it the VA. One of the Peninsula's oldest federal operations, it will celebrate its 140th anniversary on December 14, 2010. That means it began in 1870.

Few Peninsula residents, except ailing veterans of the nation's wars and their families, ever visit the VA, but it is on a beautiful site. To one side is Hampton University, occupying the pre–Civil War site of Little Scotland plantation, once owned by the prominent Segar family. On the other side is the Hampton Roads Bridge-Tunnel and the old Strawberry Banks Motel.

The Hampton VA came into existence almost by accident. In 1855, a Baptist women's college, called Chesapeake Female College, was built on its site. The building's

unmistakable dome was a help to navigators.

When the Civil War broke out in 1861, Chesapeake Female College was taken over by the army as a hospital for wounded Union soldiers sent to Fort Monroe. It was still in Union custody in 1870 when Uncle Sam, on October 17, chose it as the fourth of its newly created National Homes for Disabled Volunteer Soldiers and Sailors.

In its early years, it was full of aging veterans, many in good health. In those days, it was called a domiciliary home or asylum. The hospital emphasis came after World War I.

Records indicate that the Chesapeake College building and grounds were sold for a meager $50,000 in cash to Uncle Sam in 1870 by Benjamin Butler, the ex-Massachusetts lawyer who had become Fort Monroe's commanding officer in the Civil War.

How did that old soldier get title to a Southern college campus? Butler, you may remember, was said to have purloined much of

*Casemate Museum Collection*

**The National Soldiers' Home enjoyed a park-like setting**

**Campus of National Soldiers' Home, circa 1920**

New Orleans's silverware when his Union troops occupied that city. They called him "Spoons" Butler for that. Do you suppose there was government misconduct, even then?

Gradually buildings were added to the site in the early 1900s, and, in 1904, when a new barracks and restaurant (dining hall) were added, one visitor noted on a postcard: "Over 1000 men stood eagerly awaiting the signal to enter the hall for dinner. [African Americans] as well as whites all looked very happy. Some were very old & bent while others seemed quite active." The card said that more than five hundred gallons of soup were made every day.

In those early days the community was called Chesapeake City (and became Phoebus in 1900), and it developed saloons, gambling houses, and bordellos to attract the pension money of Soldiers' Home residents. In fact, a New York newspaper declared Chesapeake City to be the wickedest Atlantic coast town, remaining as such until Virginia adopted prohibition in 1914 and closed all saloons.

Neighbors of the Soldiers' Home in early days were the Hygeia Hotel, run by skilled hotelier Harrison Phoebus, and its newer rival, the first Chamberlin Hotel. Both benefited from

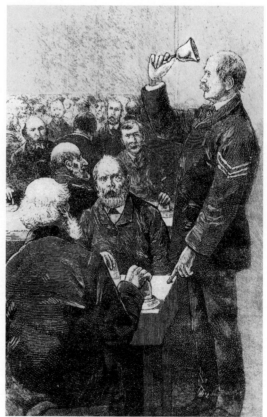

Frank Leslie's Illustrated Newspaper
**Nightly dinner bell to begin the meal**

Virginia's liberal whiskey and gaming laws until prohibition triumphed. Nationwide prohibition came later via the 14th Amendment to the Constitution, in 1918, to be repealed in the 1930s.

The Soldiers' Home took steps to ensure that its residents had a variety of recreational and entertainment opportunities. There was a billiard room, conservatory, and numerous spots to fish and boat. The old soldiers could walk easily to nearby communities or take a daily steamboat trip from Hampton to Norfolk. A theater was added, modeled after Ford's Theatre in Washington, and was only razed several decades ago after years of disuse.

Many Peninsula residents in the first half of the twentieth century would drive around the area on Sunday afternoons seeing the sights, including the Old Soldiers' Home. Great banks of blue hydrangeas and orange cannas bordered paths along the waterfront, decorating the area near the home.

The original college building, with its distinctive cupola, was enlarged and used by the VA until the 1930s, when replaced by today's hospital building.

The aimless old soldiers who used to wander about the grounds are no longer evident. Today's hospital cooperates with other hospitals and physicians and enjoys a close working relationship with the Eastern Virginia Medical School in Norfolk, the Medical College of Virginia (now Virginia Commonwealth University Medical Center) in Richmond, and the University of North Carolina's Medical School. Now, it is a 468-bed facility that serves fifteen counties in eastern Virginia and ten counties in northeast North Carolina.

In 1995, the VA marked its 125th anniversary in Hampton by dedicating a gazebo on its waterfront, built for the use of patients and staff by SeaBees and volunteers. Close by is a monument marking the spot where John Smith's 1607 pioneers first came ashore on the Peninsula, marveling at the "faire meddowes" and "goodly tall trees" they found there at Strawberry Banks.

A pretty historic spot, by any reckoning.

**Main barracks building at National Soldiers' Home, circa 1908**

# 22 Presidents Come Calling

IN THE NINETEENTH CENTURY, presidents of the United States did not travel as much as they do now and rarely did they make visits to small towns unless they had a personal connection. Such was the case for presidents Rutherford B. Hayes and James A. Garfield.

In 1878 and 1881, respectively, they visited the small, private, predominately black institute—the Hampton Normal and Agricultural Institute; drove through the adjacent town of Hampton, still recovering from the ravages of the Civil War; and, of course, arrived and departed at Fort Monroe. The presidents came at the behest of the officials of Hampton Institute, specifically General Samuel Chapman Armstrong, the first principal (president) of the school.

Hayes's appearance was for the tenth Anniversary Day celebration of the school's opening, and he made not one but two speeches at the occasion. After Hayes took office, he was appalled to find that the Bureau of Indian Affairs was riddled with corruption and set about efforts to improve the plight of the American Indians, especially the education of their young children.

Hampton Institute had been a testing ground for experiments in Indian education initiated by Richard Henry Pratt, who, with the aid of Armstrong, brought Native Americans to

*Editor's collection*

**President Rutherford B. Hayes**

Hampton to study. These activities in 1878 led to the establishment of the Carlisle Indian School in Pennsylvania in 1879 headed by Pratt. The Indians were newly arrived at Hampton when Hayes accepted Armstrong's invitation to attend Anniversary Day activities.

According to the *National Republican*, a newspaper published in Washington, D.C., printed on May 23, President Hayes and his son Webb, Attorney General Charles Devens, Secretary of the Interior Carl Schurz and his daughter, and a few others left Washington at 5:30 p.m. by train on May 22 bound for Baltimore to catch a "bay boat for Fortress Monroe. [On May 23] they attend the exercises of the Hampton Normal School." There were no presidential yachts at this time, though one was purchased two years later for the president.

Hayes's visit was not publicly announced in Virginia. Nevertheless, Armstrong made sure that hundreds of people attended, including Hampton's "leading citizens" and others from Norfolk and surrounding communities.

According to the May 28, 1878, edition of the *Boston* (Massachusetts) *Daily Advertiser* the president, having arrived at Old Point Comfort in the early morning, came to Hampton Institute at 10:00 a.m. and immediately visited classrooms and inspected buildings and "reviewed the school boys in the noon drill, under command of Captain Henry Romeyn of

**President James A. Garfield**

Afterward, the presidential party and other guests gathered with about 1,200 people for afternoon graduation exercises for about fifty-four students, who politely called upon the president to speak again.

At the exercises, Hayes had just a few comments some of which expressed personal sentiments that were years ahead of his time:

> I believe to elevate any race, we must give the women equal advantages with the men. This is done here, and for these fifty-four young men and women who graduate from here today, we all unite in praying that God may bless them.

He then returned to Fort Monroe for the trip back to Baltimore and then to Washington, D.C.

Only three years later, President Garfield paid a visit to Hampton Institute. The area was fortunate to see Garfield because he was president only four months (March to July) before

the United States 5th Infantry, the recently arrived instructor in tactics."

Shortly after noon, the dignitaries sat on the broad piazza of the Institute president's home, while others gathered under the trees in the lawn, to eat lunch and then listen to Hayes's speech. In part, he said Americans have a "great duty of educating this people lately freed from bondage, to rear them up to the full status of American citizenship. And what we have seen here shows both sides of education to citizenship are attended to here," according to the *Southern Workman*, a monthly magazine published by the school and found in the Hampton University Archives. The president concluded:

> Knowing how to work to support oneself is an important part of civilized life. The man who cannot earn a home for himself—which cannot lay up something against a wet day—is not quite prepared for American citizenship. You have learned to work. Now learn to save. If you earn $10 save a little of it. If you earn $100 save more. The difference between spending all and saving something is the difference between misery and happiness.

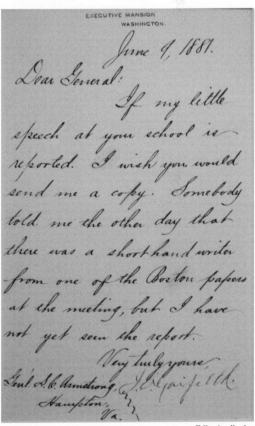

**Garfield wrote about Hampton visit in 1881**

he was shot by an assassin. Garfield died eighty days after the attack.

But Garfield was very attached to Hampton Normal, and, therefore, it was not surprising that one of his few trips outside Washington was to visit here. One of the Institute's original trustees listed in the charter, Garfield served on the board from 1870 until 1876. He wrote many letters to Armstrong discussing various approaches to educating the students, who for so long had lacked a formal chance to learn.

At the invitation of Armstrong, Garfield came down from Washington aboard the presidential steam yacht USS *Dispatch* and, on Saturday, July 4, 1881, visited the Portsmouth Navy Yard and returned to the Hygeia Hotel where he stayed the night. The next day, Garfield visited Fort Monroe and then "drove out to the Soldier's Home and Hampton Institute," according to an article in the June 10, 1881, edition of the *Boston Daily Advertiser*.

Garfield, along with daughter Mary and a son, Secretary of the Navy William H. Hunt, and his private secretary Colonel A. F. Rockwell and his wife, attended the Normal School service at Bethesda Chapel in the National Cemetery. Following the service, the president was introduced to the congregation, and Armstrong asked Garfield to make a few remarks.

In a letter to Armstrong a few days later, Garfield wrote that if any mention of his speech made the press (he was correct in thinking a shorthand reporter from a Boston newspaper was present), he wanted to see a copy.

Again, *Southern Workman*, published by the Institute, printed a story of the President's visit and remarks in which he spoke of the work at the school in educating African American as well as American Indian students.

Garfield stressed several points.

Labor must be free. And for those of you from the far west, I would omit the last word in order to enforce the first lesson. To you I would say: Labor must be!—for you, for all. Without it there can be no civilization. The white race has learned that truth. They came here as pioneers, felled the forests and swept away all obstacles before them by labor.

You come from a people who have been taught to destroy; —to fight but not to labor. Therefore, to you I would say that without labor you can be nothing. The first test of your civilization is: Labor must be!

You of the African race have learned this test, but you learned it under the lash. Slavery taught you that labor must be. The mighty voice of war spoke out to you, and to us all, that Labor must be forever free.

The basis of all civilization is that Labor must be. The basis of everything great in civilization, the glory of our civilization, is that Labor must be free!

Following the church service, the president and his party visited some of the campus buildings, according to the *Daily Advertiser*, and the dining hall, where the president "passed between tables, at one point tasting the corn bread liberally piled upon the tables." He also shook hands with various people nearby and left for lunch elsewhere on the campus. After listening to music from the Normal School choir, Garfield and his party left for Fort Monroe and returned to Washington that night.

—*Wilford Kale*

**Garfield and Hayes also visited Mansion House**

# 23  King of Hawaii Visits

HAMPTON WAS JUST A small county seat in 1881 when it welcomed an exotic monarch from overseas. He was King David Kalakaua of the Hawaiian Islands who came to Old Point by boat on September 20, after calling on President Chester A. Arthur in Washington.

Hawaii was then a remote Pacific monarchy, but twelve years after Kalakaua's visit, it was peacefully annexed by the United States. In 1959, it became our fiftieth state, following Alaska.

The Hawaiian monarch came to visit Hampton University, then called Hampton Normal and Agricultural Institute. It had been founded in 1868 by General Samuel Chapman Armstrong, a Union general in the Civil War, who was born in Hawaii, the son of Congregationalist missionaries—friends of the king.

When Kalakaua came, Armstrong, unfortunately, was away from Hampton working to bring Indian students from western reservations to enroll in the institute. The king was welcomed at Old Point by General George Getty, Fort Monroe's commandant.

Hawaii was then a struggling chain of sugar growing islands, governed by a succession of native Hawaiian rulers. However, Americans were gaining in numbers and soon took over. Especially influential were Congregationalist mis-

Around the World with a King, *1904*
**King David Kalakaua**

sionaries from New England whose descendants formed most of the sugar cane conglomerates, which came to be known as "the Big Five."

An account of Kalakaua's visit was printed in the October 1881 issue of *Southern Workman,* a monthly published by Armstrong for "the industrial classes of the South." The magazine, found in the Hampton University Archives, reflects the simple life of the Peninsula before railroads and industries.

The Hawaiian king arrived just a month before the C&O was built from Richmond to Newport News in October 1881. And he arrived immediately after the death of President James Garfield who died on September 19 from the wounds of an assassin. President Arthur received Kalakaua informally in Washington, but other Washington events were canceled because of Garfield's death.

Mildred Getty, granddaughter of General Getty, wrote, recalling the visit, that President Arthur sent the king to Fort Monroe on the presidential yacht, the USS *Dispatch.* "News that they were to be visited by a king caused excitement among the Getty family," she wrote. "At Fort Monroe they often entertained Washington officialdom, but the 'King of the Cannibal Isles,'" as they romantically thought of him, "was something else." (King Kalakaua, of course, was a

Christian, and his people had long been converts.)

Getty observed that Kalakaua "resembled President Arthur in appearance and manner." She noted he spoke English "with less accent than Queen Victoria" and "affected long 'Dundreary' whiskers, and more likely he wore a frock coat."

According to the *Southern Workman*, "His majesty was received by General Getty, commandant at Fortress Monroe (the troops of the garrison drawn up in line on the shore), and Captain Romeyn, commandant of the Normal School." The party was entertained at breakfast by Harrison Phoebus, owner of the Hygeia Hotel, a predecessor of today's Chamberlin.

Accompanying the king was William N. Armstrong, brother of Hampton Institute's president, who served Kalakaua as attorney general of Hawaii, and Colonel C. H. Judd, the king's lord chamberlain. A number of years later, Armstrong wrote a book, *Around the World with a King*, which details the journey. Critics, however, have claimed it is an embellished account and often not completely accurate.

Hampton Institute was only thirteen years old in 1881 and had few students. Among them were Indians from western reservations, who made up a large part of Hampton's enrollment until early in the twentieth century. Since then they have attended Indian colleges in the West.

Kalakaua showed interest in Hampton because of his efforts in Hawaii to train young native Hawaiians to work in the island's developing industries. Reported the *Southern Workman*, "The king, who has on his hands the problem of lifting a race into progressive civilization ... examined with greatest care the various departments of the school ... especially its industrial work."

For lunch, the king was entertained at

Around the World with a King, *1904*
**William N. Armstrong**

William Armstrong's Hampton home. Then he visited the Old Soldiers' Home, now the Veterans Administration Hospital, where he was welcomed by its head, P. T. Woodfin. After dinner in the Normal School's principal's (president's) house, the king was entertained at a concert by Hampton students in Virginia Hall Chapel. Then citizens and institute teachers met Kalakaua at a reception.

The next, day His Majesty was taken by Navy launch to the Navy Yard at Portsmouth and then returned to witness a review at Monroe. Finally he embarked at the Old Point Government Dock via the *Dispatch* for the West Coast to sail back to Honolulu.

The Hampton Institute program was to have influence on later vocational education in the Hawaiian Islands. The king was "deeply impressed with the greatness of the work and more than ever convinced that it is the only way to meet the Hawaiian problem," the *Southern Workman* reported. General Armstrong is remembered in the islands as a spiritual and educational leader.

King Kalakaua was succeeded in 1891 by his sister, Queen Liliuokalani, the last Hawaiian monarch. In 1893, the process of absorption of Hawaii into the United States began with the quiet, quick abolition of the monarchy. Sanford Dole, a Hawaiian-born American, became first president of Hawaii. Seven years later Dole became governor of the new territory of Hawaii.

Hampton's links with Hawaii remained strong through the presidency of General Armstrong, who died in 1893 and is buried under a Hawaiian stone in the college cemetery. Over the years, a few students from Hawaii have attended Hampton University, thus retaining the link with Armstrong's birthplace.

# 24 The Grand Hotels

IF YOU LIVE IN HAMPTON, you cannot escape the influence of a man named Harrison Phoebus, who died in 1886. The name is familiar throughout the area, and when one talks to old-time Hamptonians, his name invariably crops up. He ran a hotel at Old Point that was famous and, in 1882, helped bring the Chesapeake & Ohio Railway from Newport News to Fort Monroe.

Harrison Phoebus was one of the post–Civil War giants who made the area important, along with others like the Schmelz brothers, James S. Darling, and George Ben West. They started an industrial growth that accelerated with the Spanish-American War and the two world wars. They replaced Tidewater farming with shipping lines, railroads, and factories.

It is significant that Phoebus, like most of our Reconstruction tycoons, came to Hampton from the North; post–Civil War commerce in Virginia was largely the creation of Yankee capitalists.

Like Scarlett O'Hara in *Gone With the Wind*, residents of Hampton after the Civil War accepted a new commercial era as inevitable. Our industrialization has continued ever since, hastened by hot and cold wars.

Phoebus was a Marylander, born in 1840, who had fought for the Union in the Civil War.

*Hampton History Museum*
**Harrison Phoebus**

When he was mustered out of service in 1865, he went to work for the Adams Express Company of Baltimore. They liked his willingness to tackle any work, "from sweeping a floor to writing a letter," as he put it. So the company, in 1866, sent him to Old Point as its agent, handling shipments that arrived by the bay steamers that docked there.

Phoebus became a one-man industry. He was Old Point's postmaster, notary public, U.S. commissioner, insurance agent, and representative of shipping companies. Like most people in those hard-up days, he took any work he could find.

His big chance came in 1874, when he had an opportunity to control the old Hygeia Hotel at Old Point, with the backing of Samuel Shoemaker, a wealthy Baltimore friend. The resort hotel had been rebuilt after the war for families visiting Fort Monroe or seeking a rest on the wind-swept shore of Hampton Roads. It stood where the generals' houses at Monroe now stand, facing the shore and dock across a plaza with a central bandstand.

The tip of Old Point in that area has harbored three hotels before the present Chamberlin, which was built only in 1928. When Fort Monroe was laid out after the War of 1812, William Armistead built the first inn

The first Hygeia Hotel was torn down during the Civil War

there in 1820 to house visiting engineers and officers. It was operated by Marshall Parks of Norfolk. The elaborate stone construction of Monroe required out-of-town artisans who were brought from Norfolk, Washington, and Baltimore. Some ended up permanently on the Peninsula.

Parks named his hotel the "Hygeia" for the Greek goddess of health. It was a frame building with large porches, which served until demolished by the U.S. Army in 1862 to provide for a better defense of the fort, and because the government thought the large number of civilians could cause an embarrassment during the wartime. An advertisement for the hotel in the *Norfolk Herald* of 1822 declared:

> Here lov'd Hygeia holds her blissful seat
> And smiles on all who seek her blessed retreat.

The Hygeia drew Americans as well as British and French naval officers, whose sailing ships often rendezvoused in Hampton Roads before the Civil War. Old Point's historian, Dr. Chester Bradley, wrote that it "became to the planters and statesmen of the South what the Saratoga Hotel was to the North." Edgar Allan Poe recited poetry on its veranda on September 9, 1849—only a month before he died in Baltimore.

After the hotel was torn down, a restaurant —the Hygeia Dining Saloon—was built on Old Point's wharf in 1863 for soldiers and fort workers. After 1868, it grew into the second Hygeia Hotel. This was the large, red, palatial four-story Victorian structure that Harrison Phoebus took over in 1874. It stood close to the water and had a dance pavilion, bathhouse, and pleasure dock.

The first building of the second Hygeia Hotel

Harrison Phoebus installed many gadgets and luxuries so the hotel could compete with popular resorts like Niagara Falls, the Pocono Mountains, and the Virginia Springs. He put in hydraulic elevators, gaslights, electric bells in bedrooms, and bathrooms on each floor. To compete with the medicinal waters of the Virginia springs, he put in baths—Turkish, Russian, thermo-electric, magnetic, mercurial, sulfur, vapor, and hot seawater.

You couldn't help but like Harrison Phoebus. He was an attractive man, never too busy to show an employee how to do his job. He traveled to Europe to see how its hotels were run.

ton to extend the C&O line from Newport News to Old Point the next year. The village on Mill Creek adjoining Old Point at that time was called Chesapeake City, but the C&O renamed it for Harrison Phoebus. The place was incorporated as Phoebus in 1900. Later it became part of Hampton.

So successful was the Hygeia that it attracted another hotel to Old Point, the Chamberlin. Behind it was John Chamberlin, a Washington saloon and restaurant owner who was intimate with politicians of the Cleveland and McKinley administrations. The slick John Chamberlin lobbied a bill through

*Casemate Museum Collection*

**The Hygeia Hotel in its heyday, circa 1900**

"Let every man follow his bent," he used to say.

> Do not try to make a stonemason out of a carpenter or a mathematician out of a poet. If a man can write poetry, let him write it. If he can drive an express wagon, let him drive it. They are both good things.

When the C&O extended its tracks from Richmond to Newport News in 1881, Harrison Phoebus saw an opportunity to attract inland patrons. He persuaded Collis Hunting-

Congress in 1886 to permit him to build a hotel on army land at Old Point, right next door to the Hygeia.

Congress probably wouldn't have passed the bill if Harrison Phoebus had lived. However, he died suddenly of a heart ailment in 1886 at 45. He was buried at St. John's churchyard in Hampton after a funeral procession of sixty-five carriages from Old Point. *Harper's Weekly* carried his obituary, describing his prowess as a

Postcard view of the first Chamberlin Hotel in 1910

hotel man and civic leader.

As one might guess, the Hygeia without Phoebus soon lost out to the new Chamberlin, after that five-story palace opened in April 1896. Many of Chamberlin's friends came to it—Cabinet members, senators, and tycoons. *The Norfolk Herald* called the hotel "magnificent" and "among the largest and most attractive of American watering place hostelries."

Like Harrison Phoebus, Chamberlin did not long enjoy his success. He died in August 1896, four months after the Chamberlin opened. In 1902, the hotel's new owners bought and razed the adjacent Hygeia. For eighteen years after that, the Chamberlin enjoyed some of the luster that Harrison Phoebus had brought to Old Point. It thrived especially during the Jamestown Exposition of 1907, when guests included Mark Twain and William Howard Taft. Its guests made up a *Who's Who* of Edwardian America.

When war broke out in Europe in 1914, the Chamberlin went after the patronage of Americans who had once gone to European spas. It advertised,

The gouty and rheumatic population need feel no alarm at the closing of the celebrated resorts of Karlsbad and Baden Baden. At the Chamberlin, every treatment given at Aix, Vichy, Karlsbad, Nauheim, or Harrogate is duplicated.

Pretty fancy, eh? Eight years after the Chamberlin burned to the ground in 1920, it was succeeded by the present Chamberlin building. However, the new hotel never thrived as a resort hotel like its predecessors. Deprived of gambling, it had to depend on vacationers and conventioneers. The competition was growing.

In the 1980s and 1990s, a revival of the hotel was attempted, but it did not last. In 2007–2008, the massive building was converted into luxury condominiums, and the old dining room and second-floor lobby were restored to their grand appearance of the late 1920s.

In Virginia's long history as a host, its most famous hotel man remains Harrison Phoebus, the penniless Marylander who came to Old Point in 1866 as a clerk. He showed that one determined soul can create a world-famous resort. He made Old Point and Phoebus famous.

(*Top*) Nothing could stop the destruction of the Chamberlin
(*Middle*) The remains of the Chamberlin Hotel after the 1920 fire
(*Bottom*) The second and current Chamberlin, now upscale condominiums

# 25 Jewish Community Begins

THE FIRST JEWISH SETTLERS who arrived on the Peninsula came in the 1880s after the Civil War. Their numbers have steadily grown through the years—to an estimated 6,000 to 7,000 of the more than 325,000 people now living in Hampton and Newport News. Their contributions to the business and cultural life of the Peninsula, however, belie their small number.

The Jewish families on the Peninsula have made a huge contribution to local history. Their story is chronicled by the Peninsula Jewish Historical Society at the Jewish Community Center. Important to this history are more than one hundred oral histories—accounts of Jewish residents in the two cities and the other local communities—begun by volunteer interviewers in 1983.

*Hampton Public Library*

The Tignor store where early Jewish services were held

Fortunately, many of the older citizens twenty-five years ago had recollections of Jewish life near the turn of the twentieth century, and these provide a heartwarming picture of a gutsy religious minority. It's the story of penniless immigrants arriving by steerage from Russia and other Eastern European countries, starting businesses, building synagogues, and giving their all to an America they love.

The first Jewish services in Hampton were held in homes, and a congregation, B'Nai Israel, was begun in 1904. The Reverend I. K. Fisher later served as the first formal rabbi. (The first Jewish services on the Peninsula had been held in 1890 when fifteen Jewish families in Newport News rented a room above Louis and Charles Nachman's store for high holy services. In 1893, they established the first synagogue in Newport News, Adath Jeshurun.)

A third Peninsula congregation, Rodef Sholom, more liberal than Adath Jeshurun, formed in Newport News in 1915. That congregation now worships in Hampton.

In 1905, there were twenty-two members of the B'Nai Israel congregation. Services were held in a loft above the Woodson N. Tignor store, and a Hebrew School for young men had been started. In 1908, a lot was purchased and a synagogue constructed on Locust Street; the first service was held there in 1909. A celebration was held in March 2009 commemorating the 100th anniversary of the congregation. Initially, men and women sat separately in the synagogue, but about the early 1950s they began to sit together.

In Hampton, the early families of Epstein, Gold, Kantrowitz, Kirsner, Marcus, Rapeport, Goldstein, and Rosenstein settled, many in the old Wythe area; in Phoebus, the names of Ackerman, Carmel, Pear, Saunders, Newman, and Cooper were prominent.

A brief history of B'Nai Israel, compiled in 1975, states that "Mrs. Isaac Kirsner, who came to Hampton from Baltimore as a bride in 1893, remembered that the Kantrowitz Gold family had been here many years [when she arrived]." Mrs. I. W. Cooper, whose family arrived in 1902, said some of the families came into Hampton via West Point, Virginia, as a boat

Daily Press *Archives*

**Rabbi Allen Mirvis (*left*) with Alfred Goldstein**

from Baltimore docked there.

John and Fannie Cooper Ackerman settled in Phoebus, also about 1893, before it was incorporated, and they opened a tobacco and jewelry store. Her brother, Morris S. Cooper, came six years later and opened a dry goods store, also in Phoebus.

To local historians, the best part of the oral histories is probably the account of the early years when the first Jews arrived. Many of these early settlers were peddlers who came to escape poverty and religious persecution. Many of the immigrants initially landed in Baltimore and were directed to Virginia by those who had arrived earlier. Most spoke little English. Many dressed oddly.

The oral histories remember those people as "old men with gray beards and balding heads who came to the Peninsula when they were young, energetic men—in their 20s and 30s—with youthful brides and small families." Most of those parents spoke Yiddish, but not the children; they learned English.

Alfred Goldstein said his paternal grandparents settled in Philadelphia, and his parents came to Hampton in 1907. They arrived on a ferry from the Eastern Shore, after coming down to Cape Charles on the train.

In the early twentieth century, "Newport News and Hampton never did mix, like the gentiles and Jews, like oil and water. Now they want to join, everybody wants to join, but Hampton has one philosophy and Newport News has another," Goldstein said, the oldest of ten children.

Ironically, the Jewish families got along with the African American families in their area. In fact, many Jewish children could use the library at Hampton Institute and some of the professors—like those in music—tutored Jewish students at home or at the Institute.

Alfred Goldstein talked about the family grocery store; they lived upstairs and in the back with the store downstairs. The grocery opened about 5:30 or 6:00 a.m. and on Saturday nights, closed at midnight. "That was a tough business. We did a credit grocery business, a service business, open six days a week and closed on Sundays," Alfred said. The store was always open on Sabbath and only closed on Yom Kippur and Rosh Hashanah.

After World War II, the Goldsteins got out of the grocery business and purchased an existing furniture store across the street. These first-generation immigrants operated stores—all kinds, grocery, ladies' ready-to-wear, shoe—and the next generation became professionals: doctors, lawyers, school teachers, newspapermen.

Ralph Goldstein said the Jewish families were close-knit to their synagogue. There were neighbor Jewish children who did not attend the Hampton synagogue; rather their families were members of the two Jewish congregations in Newport News. "So, even though they lived [near] my house, I really didn't have any contact with those kids until high school," he said.

Now the Peninsula has five synagogues—two in Newport News, two in Hampton, and one in Williamsburg.

*Peninsula Jewish Historical Society*
**B'Nai Israel services began here in 1909**

Boom times during both world wars brought many new Jewish families to the Peninsula from western Virginia, Maryland, and the Carolinas. Ida Fenigsohn from Winston-Salem, N.C., moved to the area after World War I. "I had never seen so many Jews in my life," she said in an interview. "I thought I was surrounded by Jews. There were more Jews in one little area than in all Winston-Salem, and I loved it."

The 1930s saw the beginning of an influx of Jewish scientists and engineers into the area. They were employed at the National Advisory Committee for Aeronautics (NACA), which later became the National Aeronautics and Space Administration (NASA). The first of these was I. Edward Garrick, a University of Chicago graduate, who arrived in 1930 and was instrumental in research that helped make single-wing aircraft possible. He was chief of the dynamic loads division and, in 1972 when he retired, was chief mathematical scientist. Another major scientist was Anshal I. Neihouse, a Virginia Tech graduate, who joined NACA in 1939. His pioneer work in spin research helped develop spin recovery techniques for aircraft. When he retired in 1972, he was technical assistant in the office of NASA's Langley Research Center director.

The Jewish community provided generously for USO entertainment of soldiers in World War II. The much-admired Charles Olshansky came from the North to run the Jewish Welfare Board activities of the USO.

The Peninsula's Jewish community cherishes those early days, remembering a time centered on family life, civic spirit, the work ethic, and religious faith. Toby Morewitz, another interviewee, expressed the opinion of many: "Those were unusually happy times."

# 26 Virginia's First Golf Course

GOLF COURSES NOW DOT the Peninsula, but in 1893 there was only one—and it was the first in Virginia. It was the nine-hole course of the Hampton Roads Golf and Country Club, built on undeveloped land off Kecoughtan Road at Hampton Roads Avenue in Hampton.

Alas, the club was liquidated in the early 1920s, several years after the Chamberlin Hotel developed its own club near Phoebus. The 1893 clubhouse was torn down later in the 1930s, and the bricks used by C. Bernard Saunders as part of two nearby residences, a portion of the later development by the Armstrong family.

The 1893 club was the brainchild of two well-to-do Hampton families—the Armstrongs and McMenamins. Brothers Mathew and Richard Armstrong, kinsmen of General Samuel Chapman Armstrong, who founded Hampton Normal and Agricultural Institute (now University), and James McMenamin were the original leaders along with Dr. T. H. Parramore and E. O. Cooke. An early membership list reads like a *Who's Who* of Hampton four generations ago.

According to James M. Mayo's *The American Country Club—Its Origins and Development*, the Hampton course was among the first country clubs in the nation to focus on golf. In fact, *GOLF Magazine* lists the club in approximately 61st place in United States–built courses. The first such course was constructed in 1888 at the St. Andrew's Golf Club of Yonkers, New York.

Hampton's nine-hole course also was not the norm, Mayo wrote. The Chicago Golf Club's nine-hole course in 1892 was probably the first. Earlier courses including St. Andrew's (six holes) had fewer holes. Some had as few as four, others built seven and eight.

The 2,661-yard course was situated around what today are Kecoughtan Road and Hampton Roads and East avenues and the Hampton Roads harbor in what is now the Olde Wythe neighborhood, explained Gregory Siegel, a local history buff and member of the Olde Wythe Neighborhood Association.

He has done lengthy research on the old golf course and located numerous photographs and advertisements on the links.

The first two holes headed east to what was then woods near East Avenue, then the course went south two holes toward the water, then west one hole toward Hampton Roads Avenue with the final four holes zig-zagging among the trees and marshes. The ninth hole returned to the clubhouse where the course started. The whole area is now built up with homes.

The Hampton club built a clubhouse with the initial project, which was a concept ahead of its time. Normally, according to Mayo, the clubhouse would come years after the initial development because of the associated cost.

*Newport News Public Library*
**From a promotion for the Hampton Golf Club**

**The clubhouse of the Hampton Golf and Country Club**

There were frequent renovations, not only to the clubhouse, which also was used by the community for dances and parties, but also to the course.

Mayo never specifically mentions the Hampton Golf and Country Club in his book, probably because it no longer exists. However, it's apparent that Hampton was ahead of its time by several years; major clubs in other states did not come about until the late 1890s. By 1900, Mayo said, each of the then 48 states had at least one country club.

Tradition has it that the club got off to a bad start when its first club manager, a "Mr. Brown," angered J. Hugh Caffee, a Newport News mortician, who was a member. Caffee called Brown "a S.O.B.," and Brown sued him. Brown was represented by attorneys C. Vernon Spratley Sr. of Hampton and A. L. Bivins of Newport News, while Caffee was defended by R. M. Lett and Charles C. Berkeley, both of Newport News. After a two-day trial, the jury found for Caffee.

The club's officers were reported in the December 1896 edition of *Outing—An Illustrated Monthly Magazine of Sport, Travel and Recreation*. They were Lieutenant J. E. Shipman of Ironton, Ohio, U.S. Army, president; Matthew C. Armstrong of Hampton, vice president; and Lieutenant W. B. Homer of Brookline, Massachusetts, U.S. Army, secretary and treasurer. Other board members were George W. Sweet of Old Point Comfort and

Lieutenant J. S. Lyon of Petersburg, Virginia, U.S. Army.

The Hygeia and Chamberlin hotels at Old Point Comfort entered into an agreement in 1898 with the golf course. In exchange for helping maintain the course, the hotels could advertise golf as a recreational amenity. The first ads appeared in March 1898 before the grand "reopening" of the course on October 28, 1898, when a "silver cup" was awarded to the special tournament champion by the hotels. Most of the advertisements stressed winter golf in the South.

In 1900, the Hampton club served as host to famed English golfer Harry Vardon during his yearlong exhibition tour of the United States. Vardon at that time had won three of his six British Open championships. He played four rounds (36 holes) against Willie Dunn, the 1984 United States champion. During his play, Vardon set a couple of course records with a low score for nine holes of 38 and a record for longest drive with 240 yards on the 445-yard third hole.

Siegel said newspaper accounts reported that only about a hundred people saw the exhibition because the weather was so poor—the temperature was cold with windy conditions of up to 20 knots and ponds of water and mud throughout the course from the heavy rain of previous days. The match began at 10 a.m.

At the time of Vardon's tour, the Hampton course was described in the newspapers and each hole identified: No. 1, Vanity Fair, 234-yards with one bunker; No. 2, Great Expectations, 319-yards with one bunker; No. 3, Fool's Errand, 445-yards with a wide bunker and a ditch in the valley; No. 4, Easy Street, 220-yards with one bunker; No. 5, Rip Raps, 232-yards with a dip and one bunker; No. 6, Prairie, 363-yards, with a double bunker and clear terrain; No. 7, Chilcoot Pass, 288-yards with swamp and brush; No. 8, Hopson's

*Newport News
Public Library*

Golf Club. In 1932, he designed the well-known golf course at James River Country Club in Newport News for $500.

An early guest golfer at Hampton was President Woodrow Wilson, who came to the Peninsula on the yacht *Mayflower* and made an unexpected stop at the club on May 15, 1915. The President was on his way to New York City to review the gathering of warships assembled there for what is now called Fleet Week.

The *Washington Post* reported that the yacht arrived at Old Point Comfort with the President's pennant not flying and "consequently the guns of Fortress Monroe did not fire the presidential salute."

The president wanted to play golf with his personal friend and physician, Dr. Cary T. Grayson, who was also his military aide. A local doctor, Edward Blackmore, drove the presidential party from Old Point to the course at 2 p.m. They arrived at the club also without fanfare, wanting just to play a quiet game of golf. Wilson and Grayson played two rounds (18 holes) in a little over two hours and signed the visitors' book before leaving. No scores were available for Wilson and Grayson's play, but reports indicated the president won both matches. The men made a brief stop at Fort Monroe before returning to the *Mayflower* about 5:30 p.m.

President Wilson visited the club a second time almost exactly one year later on May 13, 1916. Jane Randolph Veneratis of Hampton,

Choice, 256-yards with a deep ditch, high brush, a wide marsh, and hilly knob; and No. 9 Santigo, 304-yards straightaway.

"During its early years, the Hampton club actively supported the growth of golf in Virginia and the Virginia State Golf Association, hosting both the State Amateur and the Virginia Club matches," the state association records said. In 1901, the club became an "allied" member of the United States Golf Association (USGA).

The top sportsman in the Hampton club was Jim McMenamin, son of one of the founders, who was Virginia State Golf Association champion in 1912 and 1913 and, in 1926, became the first golf professional at Norfolk

who then lived on Hampton Roads Avenue, apparently recalled that second visit saying,

> The presidential yacht would anchor in front of where we lived [35 Hampton Roads Avenue], and a shiny launch would bring Wilson to the ferry dock, where Manteo Avenue is now, and they would come ashore and walk down Chesapeake to Hampton Roads Avenue … past our house with about two or three men. It wasn't in the papers. We just looked up and there's President Wilson going by and it was interesting to see him, but we just went on reading, you know. It was nice that he wanted to come to this golf club.

Chesapeake Avenue, once called The Boulevard, where the golf club was built, developed steadily after a trolley line was run along the waterfront about 1904. The Armstrongs, Robinsons, Hewins, Howes, and other Hampton businessmen wisely bought up the waterfront land along the route.

A facet that nourished country clubs around the country was, in fact, the development of transportation, like trolley lines, often built by the clubs themselves or by club officers to boost interest and membership from persons out of the immediate area. Such was not the case in Hampton, however, where the two hotels helped to increase the golf business, and the trolley helped to get people there.

Another sport—baseball—had an early beginning in Hampton, when a professional team played in the Virginia League in 1896, according to Bob Moskowitz, longtime sports writer for the *Daily Press*. In midseason, the team moved from Petersburg, Virginia, after compiling a 32-60 record, and completed the season (7-30) in Hampton. It is not known where the team played.

Hampton would not be associated with a professional baseball team again until 1963 when the Peninsula Grays, considered a Hampton and Newport News team, came to play in War Memorial Stadium, located in Hampton on Kentucky Avenue, just off Pembroke Avenue.

The stadium, designed by Branch Rickey, legendary president and general manager of the Brooklyn Dodgers, opened in 1948 and was the home through 1955 to the Newport News Baby Dodgers and all other professional baseball teams through 1992. Well-known Baby Dodgers who played at the stadium included Johnny Padres, Roger Craig, and Larry and Norm Sherry. Other famous major leaguers to play at War Memorial include Johnny Bench, Gary Carter, Julio Franco, Hal McRae, Satchel Paige, Juan Samuel, Jim Essian, Lou Piniella and Gene Tenace, according to Moskowitz.

The Peninsula Grays ultimately became the Peninsula Pilots, the name most associated with local professional baseball. The Pilots won league championships in 1971, 1977, 1979, and 1980, when the team compiled a record of 100 wins and 40 losses, the first minor league team to win 100 games, and one of the greatest 100 teams in Minor League Baseball history.

—*Wilford Kale*

Daily Press *Archives*

**War Memorial Stadium in May 1948**

# 27 "America's Camera Laureate"

IN 1899, HAMPTON NORMAL AND Agricultural Institute (now Hampton University) got a big boost when a Washington photographer came to the school to photograph its students and teachers. The forty-four resulting pictures were displayed at the Palace of Social Economy as part of the Exposé nègre of the Paris Exposition of 1900. There they attracted great interest in the one-time Freed-

men's school for blacks that opened in 1868 on the site of Little Scotland plantation on Hampton River. France awarded the photographer a gold medal for her pictures.

She was commissioned by Booker T. Washington, alumnus of Hampton Institute, to document the school's success. This series, showing the ordinary life of the school, remains as some of her most telling work. In addition to the

*Library of Congress*

**Hampton Normal students working with cheese press screws**

Paris show, the works were also exhibited the next year at the Pan American Exposition in Buffalo, New York.

Since then *The Hampton Album* has been exhibited in many museums. In 1966, New York's Museum of Modern Art issued a handsome book, *The Hampton Album*, with an account of Hampton and its photographer written by Lincoln Kirstein. The book has not been reprinted, but original copies are still available at bookstores and on the Internet in hardback and paper covers.

Years later, Jeannene M. Przyblyski, art historian and critic, writing in the *Art Journal* explained,

> the Hampton images were called on to do a broad variety of cultural work. They were intended to assure an American audience that free blacks could still be counted on to take their place in the agricultural economy of the South. They were meant to reassure an international community that the United States had its "Negro problem" firmly in hand. They offered a French audience one vision of the process of cultural "assimilation" that was to be their colonial policy, in theory if not in practice.

Przyblyski also stressed,

> They provided the professional credentials for [the photographer's] reputation as a working journalist. But they also, as W. E. B. DuBois points out, could register African Americans' interest in seeing themselves.

Who was the photographer?

She was Frances Benjamin Johnston, who took thousands of pictures from 1882 until she died at 88 in 1952 in Washington, D.C. Only in her old age was Frances Johnston "discovered." Since then, she's been the subject of exhibitions, articles, and a biography, *A Talent for Detail*, written in 1974 by Peter Daniel and Raymond Smock.

Today, Johnston is recognized as the first professional woman photographer in the United States. In her lifetime she was regarded as being slightly scandalous, roughing it on photo tours, and advocating better things for women, African Americans, and Indians. She never married and left her pictures to the Library of

*Library of Congress*

**Frances Benjamin Johnston, self-portrait**

Congress, where there are more than fifty boxes of Johnston materials.

When the photographer visited Hampton in 1899, the school was thirty-one years old and had nearly 1,000 students—135 of them Indians. The students shown in Johnston's photos were learning to be farmers, nurses, housekeepers, or tradesmen. Hampton Normal and Agricultural Institute was conceived by Samuel Chapman Armstrong, a former Union general, to help blacks and later Indians learn trades.

Describing his school, Armstrong wrote in 1893:

> The thing to be done was clear: to train selected Negro youth who should go out and teach and lead their people, first by example, by getting land and homes; to give them not a dollar that they could earn for themselves; to teach respect for labor, to replace stupid drudgery with skilled hands; and, to build up an industrial system, for the sake not only of self-support and industrial labor but also for the sake of character.

After Armstrong's death, the institute grew into a university, teaching the liberal arts as well as many graduate courses. And its white professors and staff were gradually replaced in many cases by African American educators.

Johnston's Hampton photographs began with views of the school on Hampton River and of its student body, gathered in its chapel. Older male students wore the uniforms of the Hampton Battalion, identical with U.S. Army dress.

Nobody seems to have written about Johnston until she died. Since then, exhibits have uncovered many of her photographs of African American life in Virginia in the late nineteenth century and early twentieth century.

She was also interested in early buildings and street scenes. She photographed factories, mineshafts, and scenes of the West, which she took on a journey on muleback. On all these forays, she was undeterred by critics who murmured, "Ladies don't do such things." In her old age, she was called "America's Camera Laureate."

Born in West Virginia just after it declared statehood in 1863, she was moved by her family to Washington as a girl when her father became a government clerk. After attending Notre Dame Convent in Govanston, Maryland, she studied in Paris and returned to attend the Corcoran School of Art in Washington. There she developed a passion for photography and was trained by Thomas William Smillie of the Smithsonian.

As a girl, she wrote George Eastman in Rochester, New York, for his recommendation of the best camera for journalistic use. She was soon selling her work to such national journals as *Leslie's Illustrated, Harper's Weekly,* and *Collier's Weekly.*

She opened a photographic studio in Washington, D.C., in 1895, and thanks to her Washington connections, she was admitted to the White House and photographed the families of presidents Benjamin Harrison, Grover

*Library of Congress*

**Young men work carefully in a wheelwright class**

**A bricklaying class was taught at Hampton Normal**

Cleveland, William McKinley, and Theodore Roosevelt. She also photographed Susan B. Anthony, Booker T. Washington, Mark Twain, and Andrew Carnegie.

Ironically, critiques have indicated that her most famous work is probably the self-study of the liberated "new woman," a feminist ideal that was emerging about 1896 when the photograph was taken in her Washington studio. It depicts Johnston, her petticoats showing, with a stein of beer in her hand. (*See* page 82.)

Later in her career, Johnston became moti-vated to photograph architecture, often old buildings and gardens that were losing their lus-ter and falling into decay. In more recent times, historians and conservationists have looked to these photos as an important research resource. In 1928, another Virginia project—this one in Fredericksburg—consisted of a series including shacks of the poor and rundown mansions of the rich.

Hampton University owns early prints of Miss Johnston's *Hampton Album* and occasion-ally exhibits them in its museum.

# 28 All Kinds of Newspapers

HAMPTON WAS NOT A GOOD newspaper town. People read papers and enjoyed them, but, apparently, there was not enough advertising within the area to support them. The few papers that were printed in the city did not survive long, and those that did were primarily weekly papers.

The best known was the *Hampton Monitor*, a weekly operated by S. R. Dinah from 1876 to 1890. Thomas G. Elam resurrected the *Monitor*, which he ran also as a weekly, for a few years beginning in 1896. The weekly *Monitor* again resumed publication from 1904 to about 1918. It resurfaced in the 1970s but lasted just a year or so.

Prior to the first *Monitor*, several other short-lived papers operated in the city. Hampton's first paper, the *News and Advertiser*, began in 1854 and probably lasted until the beginning of the Civil War. After the war, an African American-oriented newspaper, *The True Southerner*, appeared from November 1865 until mid-April 1866. Although its publisher, D. B. White, a former colonel from New York, decided to move his press to Norfolk in February of that year, the paper was still distributed in Hampton. Two months later, his offices were attacked and the press thrown into the river; publication ceased.

Two other Hampton papers, founded to appeal to the freed population, were begun in 1865—*The American Palladium* and *Eastern Virginia Gazette*—but they died very quickly.

An invaluable paper for researchers today is the *Home Bulletin*, a weekly published from December 1884 to November 1891 by the National Old Soldiers' Home. It naturally had information about the activities at the home but also reported news of Hampton, Fort Monroe, and the surrounding area.

Down Kecoughtan Road in Newport News, newspapers had a somewhat better survival rate. Many of them circulated in both Hampton and Newport News. Those earlier papers included *The Commercial*, begun in 1881 by John Vine as a weekly. It became a six-day-a-week paper in 1894 and was sold for five cents a copy. *The Evening Journal* was established in 1899 by George W. Wood. Before the first publication year ended, it had merged with *The Commercial* and become *The Evening Journal and Daily Commercial*.

*The Wedge*, another fledgling paper, began printing in 1882 from Newport News, although some editions were dated at Norfolk. It is not known how long this publication lasted but such was the fate of many papers. Another interesting early paper was *The Thicket*, founded in 1895 by two sisters, Elizabeth and Dolly Clarke. It lasted until 1901 and focused

*William E. Rouse Research Library*
**William E. Rouse**

**Dorothy Bottom and William R. Van Buren Jr.**

on personal items and social events.

There were several early African American newspapers: the *Caret*, founded in 1895, and the *Recorder*, which moved to Newport News from Norfolk and later changed its name to the *Star*. It survived until 1941. The *Star* was edited after 1926 by well-known attorney J. Thomas Newsome.

The only known paper originating from Phoebus was *The Phoebus Sentinel*, apparently published between 1900 and 1906.

On January 4, 1896, Charles E. Thacker published the first edition of the *Daily Press*—a mere dozen days prior to the incorporation of the city of Newport News. About four years later, on April 3, 1900, the evening *Times* and the morning *Herald* opened in competition. On Christmas morning in 1901, the *Herald* ended publication. The next morning, the merger of the two papers took place, and *The Times-Herald* appeared as an afternoon paper.

In the 1890s, two Hampton citizens, brothers Henry and George Schmelz, became involved in the newspaper business. They did so in neighboring Newport News. Their papers became the long-standing morning *Daily Press*, which is still in operation and the afternoon *The Times-Herald*, which died on August 30, 1991. While the papers had their headquarters and were published in Newport News, they had a strong bureau operation in Hampton and served both localities.

Henry and George Schmelz had established local banks in Hampton and then Newport News, and had "advanced substantial sums in financing the development and publication of the paper during the first fourteen years of its existence and whose faith in its future probably saved it from bankruptcy," the Newport News 325th history volume said.

One of the stars of early local journalism was Samuel L. Slover, an employee of the *Evening Herald*, who became the publisher of the merged *Times-Herald*, which captured the vacant afternoon newspaper market. Slover left the paper in 1909 and became principal owner, publisher, and chairman of the board of Norfolk Newspapers Inc., predecessor of Landmark Publications.

Harvey L. Wilson, founder of the *Richmond News*, became *The Times-Herald*'s editor in 1902. A whimsical writer, his famous Christmas editorial, "There's No News Tonight," became a classic and was published for years in many papers on Christmas Eve. He departed the *Times-Herald* in 1909 when Colonel Walter S. Copeland and a group of investors purchased Slover's interests.

Thacker decided, in 1910, to relinquish his interest in the *Daily Press*. A corporation, The Daily Press, Inc., was established and assumed

***Daily Press*, first edition, January 4, 1896**

**Offices of the *Hampton Monitor* in 1882**

operation of the newspaper, securing many shares of stock held by the Schmelz family. Colonel Copeland was part of the Daily Press corporation, and thus the two papers fell under his editorship.

In 1913, a merger was accomplished between the *Daily Press* and *The Times-Herald*, morning and afternoon papers respectively, managed by the same corporation. At this time, these were the only daily newspapers published in Newport News or Hampton.

New corporate personalities began to appear in 1931 when William E. Rouse, a Newport News businessman who lived in Elizabeth City County, became a substantial stockholder, and his son-in-law Raymond B. Bottom, another shareholder, became president of the publishing company. In 1911, when George Schmelz died, he had left controlling interest in the *Daily Press* to his daughters. One of the daughters, Hilda, married Captain William R. Van Buren, who became a corporate director in 1932. In 1953, when Bottom died, Van Buren became corporate

president, treasurer, and news editor; Bottom's widow, Dorothy Rouse Bottom, daughter of William E. Rouse, became vice president, business manager and editor-in-chief.

William R. Van Buren Jr., upon the death of his father in 1964, succeeded to the posts of treasurer and news editor, and Mrs. Bottom retained her offices and was president of the corporation until she retired in 1981. After her departure, Van Buren Jr. became corporate president, and Mrs. Bottom's daughter, Dorothy, became editor of both newspapers. The two families presided over the newspapers until July 1986, when they were sold to the Tribune Co., with headquarters in Chicago.

– Wilford Kale

**Paperboys pose at The Phoebus Sentinel Hotel about 1902**

# 29 Montague Remembers

YOU WOULDN'T KNOW IT today, but Hampton was just a small country town until World War I, clustered around the intersecting King and Queen streets with acres of farm land surrounding it. In those days, it depended on seafood sales, boatbuilding, and water traffic on Hampton River and the adjoining Hampton Roads. Legally, it was separate from Elizabeth City County and from the nearby communities of Phoebus and Old Point Comfort. Today, the merged city has about 145,000 people.

One of Hampton's enjoyable raconteurs in those turn-of-the-century days was E. Sclater Montague, a lawyer whose roots went deep into the town. Montague described those early years in his 1972 volume, *A Hodgepodge of Memories of Hampton*, a very honest, human narrative that reflected the carefree living of pre-Prohibition Hampton. A lawyer who rose to become a state senator and a general in the Virginia National Guard, Montague knew a lot of colorful people.

"The General" and his cigar were familiar in Virginia's courts and legislative halls.

Sclater Montague (named for early Virginians who pronounced their name "SLAW ter") occasionally spoke to civic clubs about "Hampton around the Turn of the Century,"

*Daily Press Archives*
**E. Sclater Montague**

recalling people and places he remembered after he was born there in 1895. He painted a charming picture.

South King Street, now part of Olde Hampton, was one of the town's two main thoroughfares, then partly lined with shade trees. Down Queen Street, linking Hampton with Newport News, trolley tracks were laid in 1892, when the village got its first electricity. At first only Queen Street businesses were electrified, but around 1900, the power company was selling service to homes, replacing candles and kerosene lamps.

Telephones came to Hampton in 1902. "Every subscriber was on a party line that served at least five or six families," Montague recalled. "It was not unusual for the current to go off both lights and telephone and to completely disrupt both for four or five hours at a time—and several times a week."

Streets were lighted in Montague's childhood by oil lamps, ignited by George Collier. "George would ride around each evening on his bicycle, whistling," the lawyer recalled. "He would trim the wicks and light the lamps, and next morning he'd come around, still whistling, and put the lights out."

About 1900, Hampton had "at least twenty barrooms," Montague recalled, not counting

Virginia Department of Agriculture, 1928

A portion of Hampton's harbor with its fishing fleet

those in Phoebus and Old Point. "The swinging doors and stale odor of alcohol were always present." Young girls averted their eyes when they passed saloons, and his friend Eunice Skinner "was almost grown before she ever raised her eyes to see what the skyline looked like." Prohibition ended all that.

Hampton's crab and oyster houses sold their delicacies cheap then. "Anyone with an income of $100 a month could really lead the life of Riley," Montague advised. He listed the salary of St. John's Church's rector as $75 a month, of teachers as $40 a month, and of most wage earners as $1 a day. "A glass of beer or good cigar cost 5 cents. A good suit of clothes, $8 or $9."

Most Hampton whites attended Syms-Eaton, a public school that had grown out of two colonial academies in Elizabeth City County. "Anyone who had graduated from the seventh grade at Syms-Eaton was considered a well-educated and well-rounded man. I graduated from Hampton High in 1914, with 28 in our class," Montague wrote. Hampton also had the Misses Segars' School for boys and girls and Miss Bessie Fitchett's School for girls.

When Montague grew up, the legends of

Lee and Jackson enthralled most Hamptonians and spurred many to serve in the National Guard. "Confederate veterans were numerous," he recalled, "and held almost every political office." Many older men kept their Confederate rank—colonel, major, or captain. He added mischievously, "On many occasions I thought that some of them were the drunkest crowd I have ever associated with."

Hampton grew up as one of Virginia's major ports, especially during the early colonial days, but by 1900, had long lost major shipping because of the limited depth of Hampton River. The wharf on South King Street was still "a beehive of activity," he noted, as the fishing and seafood industry grew, and from the two daily round trips to Norfolk provided by the SS *Luray*, "a sidewheeler that emitted large volumes of smoke." That ship carried Hampton's seafood and farm produce to market, and allowed residents to shop in Norfolk.

The town's hostelry was the Barnes Hotel, known locally for its dining room and bar. "As I remember it," Montague used to say, "after the C&O train left Williamsburg, the C&O conductor would start announcing in each coach, 'Barnes Hotel.' It occupied a place in this com-

**Hampton Creek separates the city in the background from Hampton Institute in 1918**

munity similar to what The Greenbrier does at White Sulphur Springs, West Virginia."

After leaving the Hampton Wharf, close to the J. S. Darling oyster plant, the *Luray* stopped at Hampton Institute, the National Soldiers' Home and at Old Point before heading to Norfolk. "At least one hour was consumed between Hampton and Old Point," he remembered.

Montague was attracted by the camaraderie of Hampton's Company D of the 4th Virginia Infantry, which he later joined. He remembers their embarking for the Spanish- American War in 1898, when he was only 3. While watching the departure, he fell off a cracker barrel and cut his head so badly it required twenty-two stitches. He liked to point them out.

Montague's wife was the former Suzanne Garrett of Williamsburg and his son, David Nicholls Montague, practiced law in Hampton from 1961 to 2002 and served from 1971 to 1974 as Hampton's mayor.

According to Montague, Hampton began to grow big and impersonal in World War I. Later in the century most of King and Queen streets' buildings were torn down, making way for Queensway Mall, which saw brief success. It seemed that the aging general preferred the sleepy town he grew up in to the big Hampton of the later twentieth century. He'd conclude his reminiscences by saying, "Those days are now gone, but with me they are not forgotten." Oh, for the bygone days!

**Intersection of King and Queen streets**

# 30 The Great White Fleet

AN AGED PHOTOGRAPH in an antique shop in Phoebus seemed to look familiar. It was as an aerial view of Old Point Dock crowded with yachts and people. It turned out to be a shot made in 1909, when the "Great White Fleet" returned to Hampton Roads after a triumphal fourteen-month voyage around the world.

It's forgotten now, but, even in the middle of the twentieth century, people still talked about the Great White Fleet and its voyage. It was Teddy Roosevelt's way of letting the world know that the United States had become a great naval power.

And what a success it must have been! The Navy had painted its sixteen biggest warships white—to show that America wanted peace—and sent them to Tokyo to impress the Japanese.

They made a lot of other political stops in South America, Europe, and Asia—all to "show the flag" and let the world know that America had become a world power.

The photograph of the fleet's arrival obviously was taken from the old Chamberlin Hotel, which stood on the waterfront till it burned in 1920. It showed the Old Point dock surrounded by sightseeing boats, with larger ships anchored offshore. It was apparently taken on February 22, 1909—the memorable day when the fleet sailed through the Virginia Capes to be met in Hampton Roads by President Roosevelt aboard his yacht, the *Mayflower*. This event was just two weeks before William Howard Taft became president.

The fleet's return was a sequel to the Jamestown Exposition of 1907, from which the

**President Theodore Roosevelt's Great White Fleet steamed from Hampton Roads**

fleet had sailed on its mission with Teddy's waterside blessing. Roosevelt believed America needed a big navy to help the British navy keep world peace.

Hampton was involved because most of the VIPs attending the ships' departure in 1907 and the fleet's return in 1909 stayed at Old Point in the Chamberlin Hotel. The Newport News shipyard was also involved in the voyage, for it had built seven of the sixteen battleships—the USS *Louisiana, Virginia, Minnesota, Missouri, Illinois, Kearsarge,* and *Kentucky*—which made the cruise. Also, in the fleet were six destroyers and several auxiliaries.

United States Navy

USS *Virginia,* part of the 1907 fleet

This flotilla attracted much attention and was a dramatic looking force when it sailed out of Hampton Roads on December 16, 1907. A lot of Hamptonians remembered seeing Roosevelt arrive on the presidential yacht. Roosevelt's send-off was his third visit to Hampton Roads in that year. He twice visited the Jamestown Exposition: at its opening in April, which included an International Naval Review, and to speak again in June.

Roosevelt was great at dramatic actions. He wanted a good navy so the nation could "speak softly and carry a big stick," he said. He had seen the Japanese defeat a Czarist fleet in the Pacific in 1904–05, and he knew the Land of the Rising Sun was on the rise. As a matter of fact, Roosevelt won the Nobel Peace Prize for his role in ending the Russo-Japanese War in 1905.

A visiting minister, the Reverend Robert MacArthur of Calvary Baptist Church in New York City, was so moved by the sight of the fleet's departure past Old Point that he said: "It drove me to prayer. I could see in it America's assertion of her right to control the Pacific in the interest of civilization and humanity."

Those were simplistic days.

As the ships sailed out of Hampton Roads, Roosevelt stood on the bridge of the *Mayflower* and waved. They said you could hear the band on one quarterdeck playing "The Girl I Left Behind Me" and then "Auld Lang Syne" as the monsters sailed past Hampton and Old Point.

The ships were manned by 12,000 sailors—"perfectly bully sailors," Roosevelt called them. They carried as mascots twenty-five goats, a donkey, thirty-two dogs, two pigs, and a dozen parrots. (The Navy wouldn't allow mascots later.)

On its voyage, the fleet sailed 43,084 nautical miles. It returned under a bleak February 1909 sky, but the shores of Hampton Roads were crowded with welcoming souls. People who watched them come in have told how exciting it was to see that seven-mile long string of gunboats coming through the Virginia Capes and thence past Old Point.

To greet the returning ships, Roosevelt was on his presidential yacht with his wife, two sons, and two daughters, one of them Alice Roosevelt Longsworth and her husband, House Speaker Nicholas Longworth. The *Mayflower* stood off the shore of Fort Monroe in order that the president could receive the twenty-one-gun salute of the arriving ships. Shore guns at Monroe then fired to return the salute of each passing ship.

A witness that exciting day was William Breslow, a 15-year-old New Yorker who had come to Old Point with two teenage friends to work on bumboats that would supply incoming ships with newspapers, magazines, ice cream, pies, and other items sailors had lacked at sea. Bumboats flourished in ports around the world in those days before the U.S. Navy developed more adequate means of meeting fleet needs.

Breslow later became a New York dentist, and in 1971, then an old man, he wrote his memories of the event in a book called *Bumboater*. Sailing in a single file, 400 yards apart, the ships slowed to ten knots as they neared Fort Monroe. Breslow wrote:

> I could see that the rails were manned by officers and men in dress blue. The thousands lining the shores were cheering and shouting, but I stood silently near my bumboat. ... As each of the ships came abreast of the *Mayflower*, it boomed out a 21-gun salute to the president, who stood at attention on the quarterdeck.

The ships, after their salute to the president, formed a double column and swung around until their bows faced the Fort Monroe shoreline. There they anchored.

According to Breslow,

> The wharf at Old Point was a beehive of activity. Some 2,000 New York newspapers would arrive at the Fort Monroe Post Office [each day] to be carted down to the Wharf, where the local agent would distribute them to the bumboaters. ... When local bakers could no longer supply the necessary pies, they had to be delivered daily from Norfolk.

After the president had greeted the Great White Fleet and gone from ship to ship in an admiral's gig to individually greet and congratulate officers and crews, he rushed back to Washington on the *Mayflower*. However, the fleet remained anchored near Fort Monroe and the Hotel Chamberlin for two weeks, with sailors enjoying shore duty and leave.

During the fleet's visit, many wives and sweethearts of officers and enlisted men stayed at the Chamberlin and the grand Monticello Hotel in Norfolk, which were the centers of fleet social life. Sailors also were entertained by Hampton citizens with many parties held at the Chamberlin.

Ironically enough, the ships of the Great White Fleet were all obsolete when they sailed in 1907, although most people didn't know it then. They were obsolete because the British in 1906 had just commissioned their HMS *Dreadnought*, the first of the all-big gun ships.

Writes William L. Tazewell in *Newport News Shipbuilding: the First Century*: "The *Dreadnought* was as revolutionary in 1906 as the *Monitor* and *Merrimack* had been in 1862, and for the identical reason." That is, it outgunned all previous ships and made them obsolete.

*Casemate Museum Collection*

**The Great White Fleet sails past Old Point Comfort**

# 31 "Show Boat"

ONE OF THE PLEASURES enjoyed in bygone days by Americans living in river communities was the showboat, or floating theater, which traveled from one town to another and produced nightly melodramas.

Americans know something about them from Edna Ferber's 1926 best-selling novel, *Show Boat*. It was such a hit that producer Florenz Ziegfeld rushed to turn it into a musical comedy by Jerome Kern and Oscar Hammerstein II, which opened on Broadway the next year.

Three movies were eventually made of it, but the best remembered is the 1951 *Show Boat* version with Kathryn Grayson, Ava Gardner, Howard Keel, and Joe E. Brown. Revivals of

that show, which some critics call the finest musical in American history, have been produced on several occasions since.

Virginians of the horse-and-buggy era knew the showboat through the James Adams Floating Theatre. It was a square-ended barge that was towed through the tidal waters of Virginia and North Carolina each spring, summer, and fall from 1914 to 1941. Its two-story wooden superstructure bore big painted letters proclaiming it "The Original Floating Theatre." In fact, Pulitzer Prize–winning author Ferber spent a number of days on Captain Adams's showboat in Bath and Belhaven, North Carolina, in the spring of 1925 getting invaluable material for her novel.

After usually wintering in Elizabeth City,

*Duane E. Mann Collection*

**Captain James Adams's Floating Theatre**

North Carolina, the showboat docked at Hampton in the spring during its early years and at dozens of other towns along the Chesapeake Bay and its estuaries in its lengthy annual season. During 1914, its first year on the circuit, the showboat stopped at Hampton and forty-two other locations, according to C. Richard Gillespie's volume, *The James Adams Floating Theatre.*

It is surmised that the showboat docked at the Hampton wharf on the Hampton River because it had a shallow draft, rather than at a pier near the fort site. The wharf would also put the vessel nearer its potential audience.

Other Virginia stops usually included Crittenden, Irvington, Urbanna, Tappahannock, Reedville, and Mathews. On the Eastern Shore, it often played at Tangier Island, Onanock, and then went northward to the Maryland towns of Snow Hill, St. Michaels, Queenstown, and Chestertown.

Posters announced the showboat's coming to town for weeks in advance, but you couldn't buy tickets until performance time. When the boat was towed into town, its orchestra of four or five musicians performed on deck to alert the populace.

From all accounts, the James Adams Floating Theatre was a small, utilitarian vessel of a shallow draft to enable it to get up creeks like the Pagan River near Smithfield and the Chowan and Neuse rivers in North Carolina. The theater had about two hundred seats, a small stage, and dressing rooms for a half dozen actors. Crewmembers appeared as extras.

The earliest showboat was recorded in 1817 on the Kentucky River. Run by Noah Ludlow; it presented eleven "Great Shakespearian actors." His boat was a 100-foot keelboat, propelled by poles and oars and called *Noah's Ark.* Pleased by his early success, Ludlow moved his boat to the longer Mississippi River, where he found the populace "starving for theater."

Another early showboat was built at Pittsburgh in 1831 for William Chapman, descendant of an English theater family. The company included Chapman's wife, mother, and children. He and his troupe traveled yearly down the Ohio and Mississippi rivers, without schedule or advance publicity. When his boat reached a suitable port, Chapman tied up, his trumpeter blew a fanfare to attract a crowd, and he put on *Hamlet* or *Othello.* Admission price was twenty-five cents for children and fifty cents for adults.

One Mississippi showboat was run by a gifted comedian, Sol Smith, formerly of New York. Sol was so well received that he became manager of the St. Charles Theater in New Orleans and performed in variety theaters. In those days, theaters often accepted farm produce in lieu of cash for admission, a device that Virginia impresario Bob Porterfield adopted for his now-famous Barter Theater in Abingdon.

The Adams Floating Theatre was the first and maybe only one in Virginia. There were several others in Maryland, and novelist John Simmons Barth of writes about one in his novel, *The Floating Opera.*

*Marguerite Young*
**James Adams (*top*) and Gertrude Adams**

For a few people, it is hard to hear any of the songs from *Show Boat*—"Ol' Man River," "Can't Help Lovin' Dat Man," or "Bill"—without thinking of Captain Adams's dumpy little boat tied up at a Chesapeake Bay dock long ago when life was young.

Some theatricals have a hint of immorality about them, but the Adams troupe won the hearts of its small-town patrons because of its moral plays and its well-behaved troupe. It was run by James Adams and his wife, Gertrude, a pair of Michigan ex-vaudeville acrobats. Its leading lady was Jim's pretty sister, Beulah, "the Mary Piciform [Pickford] of Chesapeake Bay." Most of the actors were married couples who doubled as stagehands, cooks, and ticket-sellers.

It's hard to imagine a more exciting event in Hampton during that era than the arrival of Captain Adams's showboat. Ironically, that showboat sank at Thimble Shoals in Chesapeake Bay a month before the Broadway opening of the play, but the boat was refloated and towed to Norfolk and rebuilt over the winter. It returned to the Chesapeake—good as new—in 1928 and continued to delight coastal towns until it ended its long life on February 3, 1941, in Thunderbolt, Georgia.

Daily records of the showboat's summer tours, recorded in Gillespie's book, show the company usually spent six days each summer (1914–1920) in Hampton, giving a different show each night. The boat's auditorium held 850 patrons, 350 of them in the balcony.

In 1915, for example, seven plays were offered: *His Daughter's Honor*, *Tempest and Sunshine*, *Her Shadowed Past*, *The Moonshiners*, *A Woman's Warning*, *Why Girls Leave Home*, and *Wedded and Parted*. Most of them harked to the Victorian melodrama, with virtuous heroines, handsome heroes, villainous landlords, and happy endings. Audiences howled at the broad comedy and wept at the tragedy. Sometimes they hissed the villain.

Gillespie lovingly chronicled the popularity of the actors and the following they developed in those remote waterfront towns, which were entranced by the bright lights of the stage. He also follows the many cast changes as actors came and went.

Some of the information in Gillespie's book comes from Robert Burgess, former Mariners' Museum curator, and many photographs are from the museum and other art sources. The author cites more than 275 newspaper accounts of the showboat in the years of its heyday. Obviously, everybody loved that showboat.

*Duane E. Mann Collection*

A portion of an advertisement for the showboat

# 32 Hampton's Red Cross

EW CIVIC ORGANIZATIONS on the Peninsula date back as far as World War I, but the Red Cross does. The Elizabeth City County Chapter of the American Red Cross was begun on April 6, 1917, before the United States declared war against Germany.

Back then there were few Red Cross chapters anywhere, with only about 104 nationwide in 1914. But, during the war, towns across America organized Red Cross units to befriend American soldiers and their families. Hampton was one of the first two hundred local chapters.

Today the Red Cross is a year-round angel of mercy for victims of warfare and catastrophe. The nonprofit, nonpolitical agency has been headed through the years by distinguished Americans: U.S. President William Howard Taft, chairman and later president; Rear Admiral Cary T. Grayson of Virginia, chairman; General George C. Marshall, president; Ambassador Elsworth Bunker, president; General Alfred M. Gruenther, president; Dr. Frank Stanton, president; and more recently, former cabinet member Elizabeth Dole, who later became a U.S. Senator from North Carolina, president.

Hampton's Red Cross chapter, was inspired by the designation of the Peninsula as a major port of embarkation after President Woodrow Wilson chose General John J. "Blackjack" Pershing to command the American army sent

to France. To kick off the local Red Cross, Frank Darling, a wealthy Hampton oyster dealer and shipbuilder, led a parade through Hampton that ended at the foot of Victoria Avenue at the present Hampton Yacht Club.

In no time, citizens raised $8,000 for Red Cross needs. Ladies organized hospitality and sewing groups and ministered to soldiers in the

*Casemate Museum Collection*

**Red Cross volunteers meet at Fort Monroe in 1942**

half-dozen Army camps—Hill, Stuart, Morrison, and others—hastily built by the army along the Chesapeake & Ohio Railway tracks.

On July 1, 1917, about three months after Hampton's chapter was begun, the Newport News–Warwick Red Cross Chapter was formed. In 1952, the names were changed to the Hampton and Newport News chapters, respectively. After much debate and discussion, the chapters merged, holding the first official meeting of the new Hampton Roads Chapter in May 1966.

Although the Peninsula army camps dur-

Red Cross workers provided aid after the 1933 Hurricane

Volunteers also helped with the typhoid immunizations that were required throughout the area immediately after the storm.

When World War II erupted, the Peninsula in 1942 again became a port of embarkation, and the Red Cross in both the Hampton and Newport News chapters expanded their activities. The Hampton Chapter actively worked with the small chapter, primarily of women, that was established at Fort Monroe.

ing World War I—holding areas for young doughboys who awaited army and navy transport convoys—were located in Newport News along the Chesapeake & Ohio's tracks, the Hampton Red Cross did much to help those soldiers during their wait. Later, just after the war ended, many servicemen housed in the ill-heated camps died of flu during the epidemic induced by the prolonged East Coast cold spell of the winter of 1917–1918. The Hampton unit did much to relieve ailing GIs and their worried kin.

As the soldiers returned, the local Red Cross chapters turned to making the troops feel welcome back home. The local groups also assisted the French war brides who arrived on the Peninsula. They needed help, too. Some brides had babies or were pregnant, and some brought other members of their families with them. The Red Cross in Hampton helped teach English to these women.

Between the two world wars, the Red Cross was frequently involved in hurricane relief. The worst storm was the August 1933 hurricane, when water rose high all over the area and the streets of downtown Hampton were completely flooded. Hours of Red Cross work were needed to overcome that calamity.

More than a million servicemen shipped overseas from Newport News piers. Again, the Red Cross eased the pain of war and befriended servicemen and their families at Camp Patrick Henry, the main embarkation facility, and other bases. Gray Ladies in Hampton often lent a friendly hand to those "shipping out."

The Hampton Chapter, like its sister group in Newport News, started out a small, all-volunteer organization, but, as the population grew, the need for expanded services increased, and personnel had to be hired. In 1949, the chapters entered the Blood Program when Newport News Shipbuilding and Dry Dock Company and NASA-Langley became the first to sponsor local bloodmobiles.

Once the merger of the two chapters was accomplished, the combined Hampton Roads Red Cross Chapter was able to respond more adequately to crises like the June 1966 airplane crash in Buckroe, in which two persons were killed and forty-six injured, with seventeen of them hospitalized.

In 1917, when the chapters were organized, there were only about 42,000 people in the area; by 1960, it had grown to 203,000. Now, in 2009, the population is estimated at about 325,000.

# 33 Steamers Connect People

ABOUT ONE HUNDRED YEARS ago, it was the end of the horse era and the beginning of the automobile age. In the horse-drawn years, people lived their whole lives within a radius of a few miles; nowadays, many Americans cover hundreds of miles by car in a day.

In eastern Virginia, the auto also replaced a network of Chesapeake Bay steamship lines that had long served Maryland and Virginia. In those days, one could catch the SS *Smithfield* at Old Point and go up the bay or sail across Hampton Roads on the steamer *Virginia*.

Sleek white steamers then connected at Norfolk and Old Point with the larger bay liners, which plied overnight between Tidewater Virginia and such "northern" ports as Washington and Baltimore. It was slow but comfy travel.

Of all Virginia's beloved riverboats, none is more happily remembered than the gleaming white SS *Pocahontas*, which made three round trips weekly between Hampton Roads and Richmond on the James River. Along the way, it stopped at a dozen wharves and plantation docks that dotted the shores of the historic counties of the Peninsula and Southside.

A few years after World War I, the *Pocahontas* was sold, but her sister ships—the *Berkeley* and the *Brandon*—continued for a few years longer to provide nightly service from Tidewater to Richmond, though in the 1930s they quit, too.

There was something romantic about those long, graceful ships. Not too long ago, many residents along the James River still missed the "Pokey," as they aptly called her. She was a lifeline between the towns where rural Virginians then went to shop. "She could beat anything on the river," a former fireman on the ship said gleefully, and her captain, Charles C. Graves, was "the best shipper of them all." Steamboats and their skippers then attracted ardent hero-worship.

The *Pocahontas* was proclaimed a "palace

*The Mariners' Museum*

**The SS *President Warfield* alongside the wharf at Old Point Comfort**

The SS *Pocahontas* – the "Pokey" – traveled between Hampton Roads and Richmond

steamer" when built of steel and wood at Wilmington, Delaware, in 1893 for the Virginia Navigation Co. She plied the James River for the next twenty-seven years, zigzagging from one shore of the river to the other to pick up and discharge passengers, freight, and livestock. The trip usually departed Norfolk at 6 a.m., and the ship would cross Hampton Roads to Old Point and to Newport News before heading up the James.

Tidewater steamers were one-stack vessels, painted white, with a cargo deck, a passenger deck, and plenty of deck space where children could play and watch the birds fly by.

Old Hamptonians remember a daily passenger steamer that sailed to Norfolk, making a stop at Old Point en route. Old Point then had a busy government dock, with Chesapeake Bay steamers from Washington and Baltimore intermingling with smaller river steamers from places like Urbanna, Irvington, West Point, and Kiptopeke docking there. Sometimes three or four ships would be docked at one time.

A Sunday family adventure in the 1920s would be an occasional drive to Old Point to watch the big white steamers rushing in, then reversing propellers in clouds of white water, and carefully edging up to the dock so the crew could toss the hawsers to the dock.

Old Point cargo included barrels of oysters, crabs, fish, and clams, for Hampton was full of crab-picking houses like McMenamin's and oyster houses like Darling's. Sea turtles also abounded, and they were shipped from Old Point to markets up north. It was not unusual to see a half-dozen huge, live sea turtles lying on their backs on the dock.

Everyone marveled at the skill of the skippers of the ships, who could dock the SS *President Warfield* or the *Baltimore* or *Washington* without a blemish to ship or pier. In rough weather, when wind and waves were high, those captains handled their ships with amazing grace.

Steamboat docks became post offices, then small towns. In the old days, the dock master hoisted a white sheet or flag to let the scheduled river steamer know he had passengers or freight waiting to be picked up. The steamboat days created a world of their own; and that was a glorious age.

# 34 Langley Takes Off

AFTER WORLD WAR I was over, Americans thought it could never happen again. We were wrong. One night in February 1939, Colonel Walter Weaver, speaking at Langley Field, expressed the view that Europe would be at war in sixty days. Sure enough, a month later, Hitler seized Bohemia and Moravia (then eastern Czechoslovakia) and World War II was under way.

*Langley Field, the Early Years*, a picture book of the base, shows distinctly that Langley was making history in the 1920s and '30s. The air corps was still part of the army, but aviation was feeling its oats. Americans knew that it would be the cutting edge of our military weaponry if we got involved in war. Bright Langley officers like Hap Arnold, Carl Spaatz, Elwood Quesada, Bob Stratemeyer, Ira Laker, Frank Andrews, and Arnold Krogstad were showing what air power could do. All would become famous in the war.

Langley itself began in the midst of the first World War in Europe, in 1916, well in advance of our nation's entry into the conflict. In that year, military officials saw the need for an airfield to serve both the army and the new National Advisory Committee on Aeronautics (NACA) and later National Aeronautics and Space Administration (NASA).

Captain Richard Coke Marshall had come

Langley Field in the late 1920s along the shore of Back River and nearby marshes

Daily Press *Archives*

**Two wooden hangars were home for this group of biplanes at Langley in 1925**

down from Washington and negotiated with Hamptonians Harry Holt, Hunter Booker, and Nelson Grome, who had smartly optioned 1,659 acres in Elizabeth City County along Back River to sell to Uncle Sam.

To mislead real estate promoters, the army had also sent down investigators dressed as hunters and fishermen to look over the prospective Langley site. A half-dozen farms were included—Frank Darling's Sherwood, Jim Kimberley's Lamington and Tide Mill, and Robert Mason's Downing Farm among them. The most historic of all was Chesterville, where famed colonial lawyer George Wythe was born in 1726. All are now gone.

The area was named Langley Field for Samuel Pierpont Langley, an aviation pioneer who began his career as an astronomer, working first at the Harvard College observatory. He quickly moved to the United States Naval Academy as a mathematics professor. In 1867, he became director of the observatory at what is now the University of Pittsburgh. Then, in 1887, Langley was named the third secretary of the Smithsonian Institution after he began working on heavier-than-air craft.

His aircraft work produced models that flew, but he failed to develop a piloted plane. He called his design an "Aerodrome." Rather then taking off from the ground, Langley's machine was to launch from a catapult on the Potomac River. It failed on two attempts, and Langley abandoned the effort. But the Aerodrome did produce an internal combustion engine with fifty horsepower, definitely larger that the Wright brothers' twelve-horsepower machine.

Langley was a mud hole for years. One airman wrote:

> Nature's greatest ambition was to provide in this, her cesspool, the muddiest mud, the weediest weeds, the dustiest dust, and the most ferocious mosquitoes the world has ever known. She far surpassed the wildest hopes.

One of the workmen employed to build the base was a big, overgrown Carolinian named Thomas Wolfe. He wrote about it in *Look Homeward, Angel.*

In the early 1920s, the field was just beginning to take shape. It took, however, many years to civilize the place. By the late 1920s, Langley still looked worse than other military bases, which was really awful. In those days, officers at snooty Fort Monroe looked down on Langley as a disaster area. Stately old Monroe had age, tradition, comfort, and picturesque architecture. Langley had only temporary hovels, mud, and mosquitoes.

But things got better. The rise of aviation was inevitable. As one of the army's first airfields and as the seat of the prestigious NACA, Langley attracted not only daring young men in their flying machines but also skilled scientists and designers.

Locals at first regarded the bearded NACA wizards as weirdos, up to no good. They dressed and acted like kooks, and they worked at mysterious jobs. But years later, when that research produced rockets and trips to the moon, we had to take it all back. One of their leaders was Eastman Jacobs, a handsome, bearded scientist who later retired to California. He was called the mad genius.

And Langley itself made news. General "Billy" Mitchell, the outspoken air advocate, was often there in the early 1920s, preaching the futility of battleships in a war with bombing planes. Mitchell himself led the air bombardment by Langley planes of a navy ship in Chesapeake Bay, with General John J. Pershing looking on. Mitchell showed us the danger to ships in an air war. (*See* Chapter 37.)

One Langley hero was Colonel Robert Old, who, in the 1930s, led Langley flying fortresses on a series of goodwill missions to foreign countries: Brazil, Argentina, Colombia, and so on. Actually, they were trying to show off the air corps and impress the world with American might. Unfortunately, we didn't impress Hitler.

*Library of Congress*

**Samuel Pierpont Langley**

Airmen have flair, and Langley had its share of flair. Beirne Lay, who married Ludwell Lee of Hampton, was a good example. Besides flying, he wrote *I Wanted Wings*, which became a smash movie. Langley's big flying fortresses and their crews starred in MGM's *Test Pilot* in 1938, along with Spencer Tracy, Myrna Loy, and Clark Gable. A few scenes were shot at Langley, with the stars supported by enlisted men as extras.

When World War II burst, Langley was the crest of its wave. Colonel Weaver became a general and head of the vast Army Technical Training Command in Alabama. Many of those flyboys known in the Hampton community as captains, majors, and colonels moved up to three- and four-star generals. Langley was the father of it all.

The war expanded the Army Air Corps into the United States Air Force, a new service branch. In May 1946, the newly organized Tactical Air Command of the air force established its headquarters at Langley, bringing a new era of aerial readiness to the field. In January 1948, Langley Field officially became Langley Air Force Base.

Across the base, aeronautical research had been under way for years at NACA, but with the dawn of the space age in 1958, NACA became NASA, and the newly named Langley Research Center moved to the forefront of American space exploration.

Today, the Air Force base is home to the 1st Fighter Wing, the 480th Intelligence Wing, and Headquarters, Air Combat Command, which in 1992 replaced the deactivated TAC.

# 35 NASA Was Once NACA

BETWEEN THE TWO WORLD wars, many people in Hampton and elsewhere on the Peninsula looked askance at the bearded scientists at Langley Field as impractical space cadets. Those were the natal years of NACA, the National Advisory Committee for Aeronautics, which has grown into the National Aeronautics and Space Administration. Flight was coming of age.

Now, more than ninety years after NASA's birth at Langley Field, we've all learned what marvelous miracles those "NACA nuts" could create. They're opening up the universe for man to penetrate. Those weirdos have become heroes!

But it hasn't been easy. The federally financed NASA laboratories are chronically caught up in Washington politics. They also suffer from conflicts between competing factions in NASA and its governing board.

Until 1917, the site of Langley Field and NASA's adjacent Langley Research Center were low-lying farms and forests in old Elizabeth City County, just north of Hampton. Then, in World War I, the nation's need for an Army Air Corps base led Congress to choose it from among fifteen tracts considered here in the Sun Belt.

The chief purpose of Langley was as a year-round airfield, but the secondary need was as a site for the nation's aeronautics laboratory. It had been urged on Congress since 1911 as a successor to the Wright brothers' first airplane flight in 1903 and of Samuel Langley's contemporaneous research near the District of Columbia. Just when NACA's creation seemed bogged down in politics, the outbreak of World War I gave it a start by act of Congress in 1915.

Plantations called Sherwood, Lambington, Pool, Morefield, Blumfield, and Shelibank were part of the original package of properties put together by Hampton businessmen. In fact, a government document specifically states that "Political Boss Harry H. Holt, clerk of the court of Elizabeth City County; Hunter R. Booker, president of the Hampton-Phoebus Merchants' Association; Colonel Nelson S. Groome, executive officer of the Hampton Bank; and Captain Frank W. Darling, vice-president of two local banks and head of J. S. Darling and Son, the third largest oyster packer in the United States; saw a chance

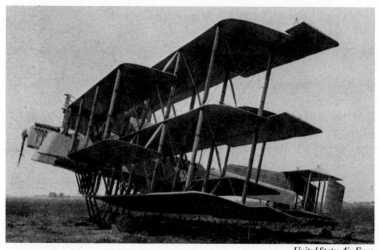

*United States Air Force*

Herbert F. John's three-engine, seven-wing craft failed NACA tests

104

to revive a dying economy, while making a small fortune for themselves."

NACA began with congressional appropriations of $53,580 for its Langley Field laboratory and $87,000 for staffing. Money went further then than now, and the original 1,650 acres of Langley cost the army only about $300,000. However, draining and filling the low-lying acreage greatly raised the cost. Many additional acres have been bought since 1915.

Hampton outmaneuvered him, and the first NACA laboratory building was dedicated at Langley Field on June 11, 1919.

By that time, Germany had surrendered, and the United States was pulling its forces out of Europe, but the army's enthusiastic air corps kept building up Langley Field. Brigadier General Billy Mitchell put on an impressive twenty-five-plane aerial exhibition there, and many of aviation's early greats like Charles

U.S. Navy Brewster XF2A-1 Buffalo sits in Langley's full-scale wind tunnel in 1938

The army launched a pell-mell effort to build the airfield after the United States went to war in Europe in 1917. One of its unskilled laborers during the summer of 1918 was Thomas Wolfe, the gangling student who would become a famous novelist. Stories of the mud, mosquitoes, and sickness afflicting the builders were told by all who worked there.

President Woodrow Wilson named Dr. William Durand of Stanford University as NACA chairman in 1916, and he chose John Victory as NACA's first executive secretary. Victory preferred Bolling Field in Washington as NACA's laboratory site, but proponents of

Lindbergh visited NACA or trained at Langley.

In 1917, a War Department engineer named Leigh Griffith was designated as the first "engineer-in-charge" of NACA and served until 1925. The title was also used for his successor, Henry J. E. Reid, but was changed in 1948 to "director." Reid's long service from 1926 to 1960 saw NACA grow into NASA and expand to other laboratories around the nation.

NACA scientists were part of the cutting edge of research that led to jet-propelled planes and then to rockets and spacecraft. Among well-known early Langley NACA inventors were Eastman Jacobs and Theodore

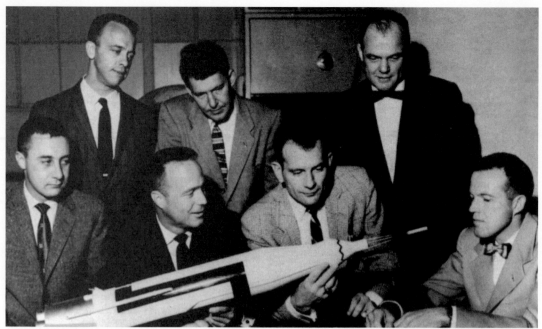

The seven original Mercury astronauts trained at Langley in the early 1960s

Theodorsen. In 1937, Jacobs received the coveted Sylvanus Albert Reed award for his improvement of airfoils used in planes. And Fred E. Weick, a NACA expert on cowlings and propellers, made propeller tests with Charles Lindbergh.

Orville Wright, the longer-lived of the two brothers who first successfully flew a plane on North Carolina's Outer Banks in 1903, remained a trustee of NACA for nearly thirty years.

Said longtime Langley NACA veteran Abe Leiss: "It never was a matter of NACA going out to find what other researchers were doing. It was a matter of other people trying to find out what we were doing."

In his interesting history, *Engineer in Charge*, detailing the Langley Aeronautical Lab's achievements, James Hansen wrote in 1987, "The engineers at Langley were so young and had not yet learned that a lot of things just could not be done. So they went ahead and did them."

With the dawn of the space age in 1958, NACA became NASA, and the newly named Langley Research Center moved to the forefront of American space exploration.

Project Mercury, the U.S. manned space effort, was undertaken as research and training focused at Langley. The original seven Mercury astronauts were trained here, and their names can be seen today on area bridges—Virgil I. Grissom, Alan B. Shepard Jr., M. Scott Carpenter, Walter M. Schirra, Donald K. Slayton, John H. Glenn Jr., and L. Gordon Cooper Jr. (left to right in the above photograph).

Shepard became the second person and the first American in space, and Glenn was the first American to orbit the earth. Astronaut Neil Armstrong, the first person to set a foot on the moon, and others in the Project Gemini space program also trained at Langley's Lunar Landing Facility.

Yes, the exciting aerial action today has moved to outer space and beyond. In the many years since Langley started, the military plane has become as old hat as the battleship. We now even take space for granted. Where do we go from here?

# 36 Thomas Wolfe at Langley

ONE OF AMERICA'S greatest novelists spent three months in Hampton Roads in 1918 and left an account of his time in Hampton and Newport News. He was Thomas Wolfe, the Asheville, North Carolina, boy who was later to write *Look Homeward, Angel* and other works, which have immortalized him since he died in 1938.

Wolfe came to the Peninsula as a boy of 18 in June 1918 to work during his summer vacation from the University of North Carolina, where he had finished his sophomore year. He was in the same class with Paul Green, who went on to become a Pulitzer Prize–winning playwright of Williamsburg's *The Common Glory* fame. Other classmates included Jonathan Daniels, a newspaperman and author, and LeGette Blythe, another multifaceted author and journalist.

Wolfe later wrote about his experiences and Peninsual events in "The Face of the War," published in 1935 in *The Modern Monthly*.

In those summer days of 1918, Wolfe knew that he wanted to be a writer. Turned down for World War I service because of weak lungs, the 6-foot, 6-inch beanpole decided to come to Hampton in June 1918 to get a civilian job at Langley. He spent a hot, uncomfortable month in the muddy wilds of rural, mosquito-ridden Hampton.

Wolfe had heard from former Chapel Hill schoolmates of high wages being paid in Virginia, so he set out, lured by "the fair promises of wealth." After a visit to Norfolk, Wolfe crossed Hampton Roads and got a job as a timekeeper at Langley, riding a horse around the field each day to record the work hours of laborers. After a few weeks' work at Hampton,

he worked briefly in Norfolk before coming back to the Peninsula to become a supply checker on the Chesapeake & Ohio docks at Newport News.

*Princeton University Archives*
**Thomas Wolfe**

THE FACE OF THE WAR

By THOMAS WOLFE

(Mr. Wolfe is the author of two of America's most important novels, LOOK HOM
WARD ANGEL and OF TIME AND THE RIVER which has recently appeared. Mr. Wo
is a regular contributor to THE MODERN MONTHLY.)

... Heat-brutal August the year of the war
ended: here are four moments from the face
of the war. One—at Langley Field: a Negro
retreating warily out of one of the rude shed-
like offices of the contracting company on the
flying field, the white teeth bared in a horrible
grimace of fear and hatred, the powerful

to kill without mercy or reprisal, the n
sun blazing hot upon the arm-band bu
the crisp shirt sleeve, and with a dull
glint upon the barrel of the squawt bl
matic that he clutches with a trembli
offering it to his blood-mad master, w
frantically—"Here! . . . Here, Mis
lett! . . . Shoot the bastard if he tr

*The Modern Monthly, 1935*

**Wolfe's days at Langley were retold in a magazine story**

"Meanwhile," writes biographer Andrew Turnbull, "he was fixing in his mind a variety of types from all over the country: Swedes from the Midwest, Jews from the sweatshops, Irishmen, Italians, Negroes, hunkies, Bowery bums." He wrote about them in his half-dozen widely published novels.

After quitting his job at Langley on July 4, 1918, the gangling 18-year-old joined some Chapel Hill schoolmates for a weekend in Norfolk. He wrote this letter on the letterhead of the Atlantic Hotel at Norfolk (actually the YMCA) on July 6, 1918, to his mother in Asheville:

Dear Mother, ... I have been working as time checker at Langley Field until the 4th. By that time I was consumed by mosquitoes and bed bugs so, upon the persuasion of several of my school mates who are working here I decided to find more lucrative employment. Arriving in Norfolk day before yesterday, I went around to the Government Employment Agency.

A young North Carolinian working there told me to go to work as a first class carpenter and told me if I would he would get me the job. So I start to work Monday at Porter Bros. who are building a big Quartermaster Terminal here. Will make about $7 a day if I can put my bluff across. Believe I can. Don't worry about me. I can always make a good living here. It is rather hard to write home after ten hours labor but I will try to write one of the family once a week. I am sunburned to a tan from my sojourn at Langley Field. My stay there was a valuable experience and I made many friends who seemed genuinely sorry to see me go. My boss out there told me I could have a job any time I came back.

Wolfe's carpentry bluff failed and he found work on the Newport News C&O piers, where troops and ammunition were being loaded for France.

The highlight of Wolfe's Peninsula summer was a visit to a house of prostitution in Newport News. He wrote of "the waiting queue" outside and described the situation:

Over the bridge, across the railway track, down in the Negro settlement of Newport News—among the dives and stews and rusty tenements of the grimy, dreary and abominable section, a rude shack of unpainted pine boards, thrown together with the savage haste which war engenders, to pander to a need as savage and insatiate as hunger, as old as life, the need of friendless, unhoused men the world over.

The front part of this rawly new, yet squalid place, has been partitioned off by rude pine boards to form the semblance of a lunch room and soft drink parlor. ... Meanwhile, all through the room, the whores, in their thin and meager mummers, act as waitresses, move patiently among the crowded tables and ply their trade. The men, who are seated at the tables, belong for the most part to that great group of unclassed. As for the women who attended them, they were prostitutes recruited, for the most part, from the great cities of the North and Middle West, brutally greedy, rapacious, weary of eye, hard of visage, over-driven, harried and exhausted.

The young writer also described in detail the C&O pier on the James where he worked as a material checker. He wrote that its cargo was "crated woods containing food and shot, provender of every sort—canned goods, meat, beans, fruits, and small arms."

In September 1918, as schooltime approached, Thomas Wolfe took the C&O to

Richmond and there transferred and went home to Asheville before reentering the university.

About twenty-five years after Wolfe's death, his UNC classmate, LeGette Blythe, coauthored *Thomas Wolfe and His Family* with Mable Wolfe Wheaton, Wolfe's sister. In the book, Mable said her brother came to Virginia partly because their brother, Fred Wolfe, was in the navy and stationed in Norfolk.

> One day someone came to Fred and told him that his brother was down at the gate and wanted to see him. Fred tells the story: "I went down to the gate and there was Tom, and with him were a couple or three of his friends. 'Merciful God, boy,' I said, 'what are you doing here?'
>
> "Tom introduced me to his buddies. 'We're working at the army [air corps] base [Langley],' Tom explained. He said that they had already been there four or five days, but this was the first opportunity he had to visit me."

Fred Wolfe took Tom and his friends to dinner on the base.

Mable, I'll never forget the meal those boys ate. It seemed to be that they were actually famished. I doubted that they'd had a square meal since getting to [Virginia]. They were probably waiting for their first pay check.

Mable recalled, "Tom tells about this incident, of course, in *Look Homeward, Angel*. It is to me another substantiation of my contention that Tom was always a youth possessed of a great pride."

Wolfe's first play, *The Return of Buck Gavin*, was produced by the Carolina Playmakers in March 1919, soon after World War I ended. His writing then led him to Harvard and New York, where *Look Homeward, Angel*, was published in 1929. In the next nine years, he produced a torrent of short stories and novels. His death at 38, following an operation at Johns Hopkins in 1938, ended his meteoric career, although several other novels were published posthumously.

So far as Wolfe's biographies show, he never came back to the Peninsula.

Daily Press *Archives*

**Langley Field was muddy and rugged in Wolfe's day**

# 37 General "Billy" Mitchell

"BILLY" MITCHELL'S IS A NAME that looms large in the history of aviation. It was "Billy"—Army Brigadier General William Lendrum Mitchell—who tried to convince the army and navy in the 1920s that airpower was all-important militarily. He made such a fuss that he was court-martialed and demoted to colonel. Then he resigned from the army.

Mitchell was a desk-bound army major in Washington before World War I, and he felt the urge to fly. He commuted each weekend by Chesapeake Bay steamer from Washington to Old Point to learn flying at the Atlantic Coast Aeronautical Station at Newport News

Boat Harbor. Buffalo, New York, airplane builder Glenn Curtiss started the field in 1915 to train flyers.

A dashing figure, Mitchell gained most of his military flying experience at Langley Field, which the army built in 1917 as a pioneer air corps base. In 1920, when aviation leaders dedicated the new Langley Memorial Aeronautical Laboratory—predecessor of today's National Aeronautics and Space Administration—Mitchell led a twenty-five-plane formation over Langley as part of the celebration.

Throughout his life, Mitchell made himself a nuisance by promoting airpower. Tall and thin, he was in demand as a speaker and wrote

*Milwaukee County Historical Museum*

**Army Brigadier General William Lendrum "Billy" Mitchell**

two books, *Winged Defense* and *Skyways*. He urged the need for strategic bombing, airborne infantry units, and polar air routes. His proposals unfortunately created strong division between military men, even after his ship bombardment experiments off the Capes.

As author Burke Davis wrote,

> No warship had ever been sunk from the air, and but for Billy Mitchell and his young men, few believed that a battleship could be destroyed by planes. Bombsights were primitive, the largest American bomb weighed 1,100 pounds, and the attack plans were untested. In the face of all of this, Mitchell created the First Provisional Air Brigade, based at Langley Field.

Writing in his book, *The Billy Mitchell Affair*, Davis, who lived for many years in nearby Williamsburg, described Langley as

> a sleepy post with seven instructors and eight or nine students when he began, but Mitchell quickly changed it. He literally stripped the Air Service of available pilots and planes at every post, flying them as far as Texas, until he had about 1,000 men and 250 planes at [Langley].

Activity moved so quickly that pilots were practicing bombing a cardboard battleship target situated in a nearby salt marsh. Within a matter of weeks, Mitchell and his crews began practicing with heavier and heavier bombs. Success followed success, and ultimately he was able to get authorization for the 1921 experimental bombing of obsolete ships in the Atlantic Ocean off

the Virginia Capes. Most of the hulls were of German warships that had been captured by the U.S. Navy in World War I.

The tests were conducted by his Provisional Air Brigade at Langley Field and Naval Air Service seaplanes from Norfolk. After the German hulls were sunk, planes from Langley

*United States Navy*

**Phosphorus bomb hits the USS *Alabama* in September 1921**

Field sank three obsolete American battleships. Later, three American ships served as targets.

After the initial phase of the tests concluded against a German vessel "with real bombs," there was much excitement at Langley,

General John J. Pershing (*second from right*) listens to Mitchell at Langley

which "roared after dark," Davis wrote.

> As Mitchell recalled it: "That night all our
> men had returned safely after their first
> great experience in bombing. Their rejoic-
> ing was tremendous. They knew now that
> unless something most unusual happened
> it would be proved for all time that aircraft
> dominated seacraft."

Davis also wrote that, during the later
phase of attacks on old U.S. vessels, Mitchell
arranged for the first-of-its-kind night attack
"launched from Langley about ten-thirty under
a half-moon." The ship, the USS *Alabama*, was
tethered near Tangier Island in the Chesapeake
Bay about forty-eight miles from Langley. The
vessel was hit on that night bombing run and
finished off three days later in a daylight attack.
One observing officer noted that this night test
"proves beyond all questions that surface ships
are menaced from the air more seriously than
had been anticipated."

The bombing success, however, did not
change the army's and navy's views of aviation
in warfare. Mitchell's Provisional Air Brigade
was ordered disbanded. Davis wrote of
Mitchell's farewell to his men: "Sorrowfully we
broke up this splendid little air force. Never
again except after another war shall we have
such experience and efficiency."

Tough-talking "Billy" Mitchell felt he had
proved the wisdom of creating an aviation arm
equal in status to the army and navy, and he
urged Congress to do so. But his criticism of
the nation's military leaders for "neglecting" airpower led to his court-martial in 1925 and his
resignation from the army the next year.

In his last decade, Mitchell was a lonely
man. He died in 1936. Unfortunately, he didn't
live to see his dreams realized in World War II
and afterward, when Congress, utilizing the
former U.S. Army Air Corps, created the U.S.
Air Force—coequal with the army and navy.
Langley Field became one of its most important
bases, today headquarters of the U.S. Air Force's
Air Combat Command and home to the 1st
Fighter Wing.

# 38 The Airship *Roma* Disaster

THE MOST INTERESTING CRAFT at early Langley Field were dirigibles. In the early days of air travel, both the army and navy experimented with the lighter-than-air craft, which Count Ferdinand von Zeppelin had pioneered in 1900 in Germany. The big zeppelin hangars at Langley attracted many Sunday visitors, who distinctly remembered the smell of chemicals and rubber in those vast halls—a very different smell from the banana oil and gasoline of the airplane sheds.

Following World War I, a variety of dirigibles were obtained by the army from British, French, and U.S. sources, and plans were made to operate them from either Fort Bliss in Texas or Langley Field in Hampton. The first such army airship was the A-4, operated primarily at Langley until it was transferred to the new Balloon and Airship School at Fort Scott, Illinois.

Undoubtedly, the crash of the Langley-based dirigible *Roma* had something to do with the decline of such experiments at the base.

Almost as appalling as the famous explosion of the dirigible *Hindenburg* at Lakehurst, New Jersey, in 1937, in which thirty-six persons were killed, was the explosion at Norfolk on February 21, 1922, of an Italian-built zeppelin, the *Roma*. In the crash, thirty-four of its forty-five passengers—army personnel and civilians—were killed.

The *Hindenburg* disaster is better known because of its spectacular newsreel coverage. The startling *Hindenburg* scene is frequently shown on TV today, and Herbert Morrison's plaintive words, "Oh, the humanity!" have gone down in radio broadcasting history.

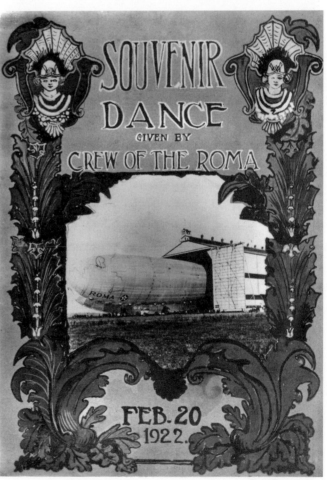

Daily Press *Archives*

**Dance program from the eve of the *Roma* crash**

113

*Roma* **crew members pose before Italy trip**

The *Roma* disaster was largely a Peninsula affair, for the airship was based at Langley Field and carried many Peninsula residents on her fateful flight. In fact, the dead were brought to Newport News for identification, and a mass memorial service was held three days later at the Newport News Casino with Langley airmen dropping roses from the air on the 2,000 mourners.

After the burned bodies were brought to a local funeral home, they were examined for identification by Dr. J. Hughes Mabry, the attending physician. The last body brought in proved to be that of his brother, Captain Dale Mabry, the *Roma*'s maneuvering officer.

How did an Italian airship get to Langley Field, and why did it crash at Norfolk?

The answer was that the army's ambitious young air service had been encouraged by General "Billy" Mitchell to acquire the ship and experiment with lighter-than-air flight. The

**Airship *Roma* rests on the ground at Langley Field not long before its fatal flight**

*Roma* was the largest semirigid airship ever built, stretching 410 feet and rising 82 feet from its personnel gondola below to its top surface. She was fueled by hydrogen, a highly flammable gas. The cigar-shaped silver vessel had originally been built for Italian businessman Celestino Usuelli, who had intended it to carry passengers across Europe, but sold it.

The army sent three Langley Field officers and five enlisted men to Rome in February 1921 to test *Roma* and bring her back to Virginia.

Daily Press *Archives*

**The *Roma* makes a landing at Langley Field**

After several trial flights, interrupted by worrisome engine failures, the deal was concluded in Italy at a price tag of $225,000. The *Roma* was disassembled and shipped by freighter to Norfolk and from there was barged in pieces to Langley Field and reassembled in August 1921.

Ominously, the Langley assemblers found that the outer envelope of the *Roma* was badly mildewed. It had to be thoroughly cleaned and patched.

The *Roma* stayed for almost a year in a big hangar at Langley, visited by thousands who were able to go on the field and view the flying machine. Smaller dirigibles were in a hangar nearby. Smoking near the hangars, of course, was prohibited because of the highly flammable fuel.

Throughout the winter of 1921–1922 the *Roma* was tested and discussed. Technical problems beset the huge airship from the start. Her engines were poor, and the craft was dangerous. Today, the safety standards of the military services would reject her, but airmen in 1922 were daredevils.

The *Roma*'s maiden voyage at Langley on November 15, 1921, was fine except for a broken propeller. But the ship missed her first scheduled christening ceremony at Washington's Bolling Field on December 17, because her engines failed to start. The ceremony was rescheduled for four days later. That day, the arrival at Bolling was delayed by several hours by the shutdown of three engines. Then, the weather began to close in, and the *Roma* hurried back to Langley with only one engine fully operable.

What would be the *Roma*'s last flight was scheduled for February 21, 1922, over Hampton Roads to Norfolk and returning. By this time, her crewmen were growing alarmed. "When we go up Tuesday, we're not coming back," Sergeant Marion Beall told a friend. Nevertheless, crew members, their ladies, and other Langley flyers staged a dance the night before as a gala sendoff.

The fatal flight, begun at 1:45 p.m., took the *Roma* over Hampton, then across Hampton Roads to Willoughby Spit and the Naval Air Station, and was headed to the Norfolk Army Quartermaster Intermediate Depot for a scheduled stop. Lieutenant Byron T. Burt Jr., who was aiding Captain Dale Mabry at the helm, reported: "Soon after we left Langley Field the ship was having trouble in keeping her head up.

**Crowd gathers at crash site**

I tried the controls repeatedly but she answered very badly."

About forty-five minutes into the flight, the *Roma* pitched forward at a steep angle. Her nose began to crumble inward, while the tail assembly twisted to one side. The alarmed crew threw sandbags overboard, but the dive continued. Mabry ordered the ship's engines stopped, but she dropped lower, striking power lines. The dirigible's hydrogen ignited, and gasoline on board contributed to the burning inferno.

**Several hours after the crash, people still look for victims**

Though the *Roma* was still several hundred feet in the air, many crewmen jumped to earth, most of them killed by the impact. Only eleven emerged alive from the wreckage: civilians Ray Hurley, Charles Dworack, and Walter McNair; enlisted men Joseph Biedenbach, Harry Chapman, Albert Flores, and Virdon Peek; and officers Walter Reed, Byron Burt, Clarence Welch, and John Reardon.

All future U.S. operations with airships would be required to use helium instead of hydrogen as its fuel, Congress directed.

The *Roma* catastrophe, followed fifteen years later by the *Hindenburg*, largely put an end to the use of dirigibles. By World War II, only the navy employed them, but they were small, nonrigid craft called "blimps," used for antisubmarine patrol and escort service.

# 39 "Sinful" Phoebus

PHOEBUS—THE FEISTY LITTLE town that became part of Hampton when that city and Elizabeth City County merged in 1952—was, at the turn of the twentieth century, called *Sin City*.

Fifty-two saloons were listed in Phoebus in 1900 by *Hill's Directory*, while nearby Hampton had only twenty-three. Most of Phoebus's saloons flourished until 1914 when the Commonwealth of Virginia moved to end excessive public drinking by outlawing all bars and saloons. The law was a harsh blow to Phoebus and neighboring Hampton.

In 1920, the Eighteenth Amendment was passed prohibiting the sale, manufacture, and transportation of alcohol for consumption. From 1920 until its repeal in 1933, all liquor activity was quiet, and speakeasies replaced saloons and bars.

With the National Soldiers' Home nearby, the many aging veterans were offered a wide choice of saloons and bordellos before Prohibition. These diversions were only a brief walk away.

Houses of prostitution, scattered through the town, also catered to the lonely veterans as well as seamen and sailors whose ships called at Hampton Roads. One publication at the time called Phoebus "the most dangerous port on the Atlantic seaboard."

In 1898, soldiers from Fort Monroe engaged in what one Hampton history calls "a bloody brawl" outside one "House of Entertainment." Fort Monroe officers finally quelled the

*Hampton History Museum*

**Mellen Street, looking east, was still dirt about 1900 with trolley tracks down the middle**

riot, and sent twenty soldiers to the hospital and seventy-five others to the guardhouse.

Phoebus grew up as Chesapeake City in the late nineteenth century following the Civil War. A business area developed along Mill Creek with Mellen Street as its main stem, leading carriages and early motorists to the bridge onto Fort Monroe.

Chesapeake City was a farming and fishing village until the 1880s, when the railroad was extended there. The line, which lasted until 1954, served Fort Monroe and the Hygeia Hotel at Old Point—where Continental Park now stands, facing the waterfront. It also had a dance pavilion, pleasure dock, and bathhouse.

Phoebus's Hygeia was special and offered luxurious features reminiscent of then-popular resorts at Niagara, the Poconos, and the Virginia Springs. These included hydraulic elevators, gaslight and electric bells in bedrooms, and bathrooms on each floor. It also

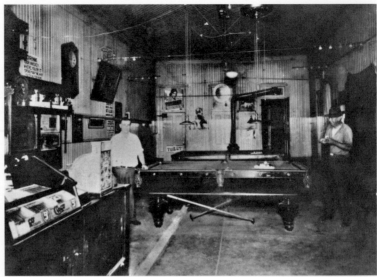

*Hampton Public Library*

**Godfrey's Pool Room on South Mallory Street in the 1920s**

offered "Turkish, Russian, thermo-electric, magnetic, mercurial, sulfur, vapor, and hot sea-water baths."

The hotel owner-manager, Harrison Phoebus, built a handsome house for his family at Strawberry Banks, across Mill Creek from his hotel.

Another Phoebus landmark—The American Theatre—on Mellen Street, was built in 1908 as a "high-class motion picture and vaude-

*Hampton History Museum*

**A Chinese laundry, barber shop, and drug store were on Mellen Street in the 1890s**

ville house." Originally there were six hundred seats on two levels. Best remembered for its ten-cent movies, it later became an X-rated adult movie theater before it was renovated and restored in the late 1990s by the Hampton Arts Foundation.

A pleasant residential street grew up out-side the saloon area and the "red light district." Many of the early residents were hired by the National Soldiers' Home, the army at Fort Monroe, and Hampton Institute.

Phoebus has changed since those boozy "Sin City" days. No Veterans Administration Medical Center patients disport themselves there now. In fact, downtown Phoebus is a tame affair compared with earlier years. Many of the stores have become boutiques, antiques stores, and artisan shops that cater to a wide variety of customers, including the tourists who daily visit Fort Monroe or other sites in the region.

Until a few years ago, a large fish-processing plant occupied a prominent site alongside the old bridge across Mill Creek to Old Point Comfort, but the Chesapeake &

Ohio Railway terminus nearby is gone. Once it served travelers from the Great Lakes who came in the winter to stay at Phoebus's Hygeia Hotel and its competitor, the first Chamberlin Hotel.

Gone also is the trolley line that used to run from Hampton through Phoebus and across the bridge to Old Point Comfort. From the 1890s until World War II, travelers could ride the streetcar from Hilton all the way through Newport News, Hampton, and Phoebus to Old Point Comfort or Buckroe. Many travelers coming by bay steamer from Washington or Baltimore to Old Point debarked there and boarded the streetcar.

In 2006, the town's historic district, basi-cally on Mellen and Mallory streets, was placed on the National Register of Historic Places by the National Park Service. It encom-passes eighty-six acres and 426 buildings, including a number of homes, many of which will qualify for a combination of federal and state tax credits for qualified preservation and/or rehabilitation.

*Hampton History Museum*

**A Fuller's Hotel sign read "Eat Lunch Dirt Cheap"**

# 40 Oyster Boom and Bust

MANY OLDER RESIDENTS of the Tidewater of eastern Virginia are saddened by the rapid dissolution of Virginia's oyster industry, which once thrived throughout the Chesapeake Bay and its tributaries. It is just one more loss to the local economy over the last half-century for an area that has lost much of its fisheries and farm income along with its boat building, railroading, and waterborne shipping.

It is true that oystering, which has been dying since World War II, had been on its last legs for years with no rebound in sight, except for the possibility of oyster aquaculture in protected trays on the bottoms of the rivers and creeks.

Watermen, who once reaped a good reward for wintertime oyster-tonging, have had to turn to other endeavors. Two virulent oyster diseases—called Durmo and MSX—have ravaged once-rich underwater oyster bottoms that for years made Virginia's Lynnhavens, Bluepoints, and York River oysters famous the world over.

Over-harvesting combining with disease has wreaked havoc on the lives of hundreds of watermen and their families in Virginia and Maryland. Catch records over the past century show a steady decline in annual volume. Once, oyster shippers like J. S. Darling and James Mallory Phillips (the "black oyster king") of Hampton sent their big fleets of buy-boats onto the Chesapeake Bay oyster grounds in season (September through April) to pay freelance tongers big-time cash for their day's catch. Now all that's gone.

Darling's success in oysters could easily be

*Hampton History Museum*

**Oyster tongers seek the bivalves on the edge of the bay**

**Large buy-boat picks up oysters from a waterman**

measured by anyone passing his oyster plant, because the pile of oyster shells grew in correspondence with the year's success. One postcard of his mountain of oyster shells said there were "200,000 bushels" in the pile.

Oystering was always a chancy life, even when our colonial forebears grappled for them in the eighteenth century. Virginia watermen tussled with Marylanders even before the American Revolution over harvesting rights in the Potomac River. Maryland watermen complained so loudly over Virginia's lion's share of oyster bottoms under a 1668 compact between the two colonies that George Washington hosted a conference at Mount Vernon between the two states in 1785. New rules were drawn up, but they didn't end the quarrels.

The worst "oyster wars" of the Chesapeake Bay erupted after the Civil War, when an inflated market for oysters led many more men into the waterman's life. In those Reconstruction years, many rural Virginians and Marylanders left farming to build oyster boats

and take to the waters. Some Northern watermen also came south.

Hampton and Norfolk in the nineteenth century became Virginia's oyster capitals, while the rival town of Crisfield arose on the Eastern Shore as the main seafood producer in Maryland. A smart Eastern Shoreman named John Crisfield (the town was named for him) organized the Eastern Shore Railroad down that Peninsula to ship mountains of oysters, crabmeat, and fish northward daily. Later, bushels of farm products, primarily vegetables grown in those "gardens by the sea" followed the same route.

After the governments of Virginia and

Maryland began renting out oyster rights in tidal waters to firms and individuals, oyster "piracy" reared its ugly head. The "pirates" would tong illegally in private oyster beds on

**Log canoes at dock on Hampton Creek, 1916**

the river bottoms. In this period both Virginia and Maryland created fisheries commissions and dispatched armed patrol boats to enforce laws against poaching.

Oystermen from the two Chesapeake states also poached on each other's oyster rocks, lead-ing to further conflict between the two. In 1883, the Virginia "oyster police" schooner *Tangier*, was fired on by twenty-five Marylanders armed with repeating rifles, and forced back to port in Onancock. Oystermen and lawmen in those days were frequently killed in "oyster wars."

An oyster boom in 1884 brought out a huge fleet of 700 oyster boats on the Chesapeake Bay, manned by 5,600 water-men. Most were poor men, both African Amer-ican and white, induced

into oystering by promises of big money. Often, the poor crewmen were locked below deck at night to prevent their escape. In Maryland, many were penniless Irish, Italian, or German immigrants who had signed up in Baltimore when other jobs could not be found.

The rapid consump-tion of oysters in the prosperous 1880s led to drastic declines. By 1892, more than half the oyster-packing houses in Virginia and Maryland closed for lack of oysters.

The Virginia Com-mission of Fisheries (now the Virginia Marine Resources Commission) in this century sought desperately for a police patrol system to protect the diminishing oysters in the Chesapeake Bay and its tributaries. Today, the Commission guards all saltwater species of finfish and shellfish and has turned to fisheries management plans to develop rules and regulations that would allow watermen to work and still attempt to protect

**More modern oyster boats work in the waters of Hampton**

those diminishing resources.

The commission established a research laboratory, initially at Yorktown and later at Gloucester Point before World War II, now known as the Virginia Institute of Marine Science, which is administered as part of The College of William and Mary. VIMS continues to measure seafood catches and tries to find scientific ways to halt their decline.

Hampton's Richard Armstrong is the only Peninsula resident to serve as commissioner of fisheries of what is now the Virginia Marine Resources Commission. Armstrong, nephew of General Armstrong of Hampton Institute fame, headed the fisheries agency from December 3, 1931, until March 19, 1938, succeeding several commissioners from the Northern Neck. He was followed by Eastern Shore residents, including William A. Pruitt of Tangier Island, the

*Virginia Marine Resources Commission*
**Richard Armstrong**

longest-serving commissioner, until 2006, when Steven G. Bowman of Smithfield was named commissioner.

Not until after World War II did oystering regain a brief strength and prosperity. Since then, nearly all Chesapeake fisheries have declined—oystering most of all. In a study published in 1981, journalist John Wennersten of Maryland sadly concluded that "The oystermen of the Bay country are being overwhelmed by the problems of an urban technological society, and their passing will be scarcely noticed."

Several Virginia watermen in recent years have lamented the demise of the commercial fishing industry and have said that "anyone looking for a way to earn a living, should run as far away from the water as possible. And that means my children and grandchildren."

*Editor's collection*
This 1920 postcard shows about 200,000 bushels of oyster shells at Hampton plant

# 41 Buckroe Beach Resorts

JUST IMAGINE, NOW, upwards of 30,000 people crowding Buckroe Beach on a July 4th or Labor Day weekend in the 1910s, when the swimming resort celebrated holidays back in the Model T era. For local residents, Buckroe in those days was the holiday resort that the Outer Banks and parts of Virginia Beach are today.

Established in the 1880s, it gained greatly in attendance when the Buckroe, Phoebus, and Hampton Railway Company was formed to serve those areas by trolley. After a series of Peninsula trolley mergers, even Chesapeake & Ohio trains began to use the trolley lines to bring excursions to Buckroe, all the way from upland Virginia.

Like other city railways in the pre-auto era, the Peninsula firm created Buckroe as a recreation destination, complete with hotel, bathhouses, and day-and-night excitement. Similarly, the C&O laid tracks from its Phoebus depot that brought thousands of Sunday school youngsters each summer for picnics, some coming from as far as Cincinnati.

America was changing in Buckroe's years.

Until the 1880s, few Americans had ventured to bathe or swim outdoors for reasons of modesty or health. Then, the European vogue for salt-water reached America.

In 1883, Mrs. Margaret Herbert opened the first "boarding house for summer guests" on the beach adjoining Buckroe's forest, but the beach had only twenty-five year-round families before World War I. The big buildup came before America entered World War II in 1941.

The beach got its name from English settlers, who named it for Buckrose in Yorkshire, England. The name came from the Anglo-Saxon *bok-cros* or *buk-cross*, signifying a cross made from beechwood—called *bok* in Old English.

Eighteenth-century Buckroe was a plantation early owned by the Selden family and later by the Armisteads. There was born Mary Armistead, mother of President John Tyler. Early in the Civil War, the Confederacy built large wooden boxes on the beach at Buckroe in which to evaporate seawater for salt, greatly needed by the South in wartime.

The beach at Buckroe was occasionally the site of illegal nineteenth-century duels, since it was distant from police. Two well-known Hamptonians, James Barron Hope and John Pembroke Jones, dueled with pistols there on April 26, 1849, but both recovered from wounds and later became friends. Hope subsequently moved to Norfolk and founded a newspaper, while Jones, a Hampton

*Hampton Public Library*

**The Buckroe Hotel was the pride of the resort community**

lawyer, owned extensive land.

Because of its exposure to the Chesapeake, Buckroe has always suffered in hurricanes. It was badly damaged on August 23, 1933, when hit by the most severe Chesapeake storm in the twentieth century. Waves reached as far inland as the present Mallory Avenue, and army trucks from Fort Monroe had to evacuate people from beachfront cottages. The damaged resort was soon rebuilt with more and larger cottages.

A second storm nearly leveled Buckroe on March 7, 1962. It was the Ash Wednesday "Nor'easter." Army helicopters evacuated forty residents, and many residences were badly damaged.

In the 1920s and '30s, the years between the wars, Buckroe was at its height. Those were the years of bathing-beauty contests, family picnics, and fireworks displays on July 4th and Labor Day.

Adding to the summer excitement was the arrival of excursion trains from farther up the C&O line: Richmond, Huntington and Charleston, West Virginia, Ohio, and beyond. The big steam engines towed their passenger cars right to the foot of Buckroe's Pembroke Avenue and Resort Boulevard, alongside the amusement park.

Before World War II, Buckroe also often overflowed with Sunday school picnickers from nearby cities, who also arrived aboard trains that stopped close to the waterfront, adjoining the green-and-white pavilion. That covered area contained dozens of tables and benches, where picnickers enjoyed fried chicken, deviled eggs, Smithfield ham sandwiches, and iced tea.

At night, the pavilion offered dances at ten cents each or three for a quarter.

For grownups, the Buckroe Hotel offered good "shore plates" at modest prices. Fried spot

was a favorite, together with croaker, deviled crabs, clam fritters, scalloped oysters, and cornbread. (Southern cuisine dictated that cornbread be eaten with seafood.)

An early feature of Buckroe was its penny arcade, where you watched short, silent movies

Daily Press *Archives*

**Buckroe Beach welcomed bathers in 1910**

for five or ten cents apiece—bits of Mack Sennett comedy or Charlie Chaplin melodrama. It was all good, clean, family fun—maybe a hoochie-coochie dance but nothing more.

Then there were "games of skill" operated in booths at ten cents a chance or three for twenty-five cents. The chance might be hitting a target with a BB gun or knocking down a wooden Indian with a baseball. The "prize" was a cheap bisque kewpie doll with a brightly colored dress or feathers. If you won, the kewpie went to your girlfriend. (It looked great at first, but awful later.)

In those Prohibition days, booze was rarely evident at Buckroe. Instead, the management pushed orange juice for the thirsty at various stands or even a mix of orange juice and cod liver oil. Buckroe patrons bought orange juice drinks as if they were the very elixir of life.

But the real thrill for Buckroe teenagers came from the rides—the merry-go-round, the Old Mill Stream, and the "leapty-dips," as roller coasters were often called.

A large excursion train parks at Buckroe bringing passengers to the beach resort

The merry-go-round was the choice of smaller children, for it had rousing carousel music and brightly colored horses that leaped and rocked. In that era of innocence, it seemed sophisticated and exciting, especially when a child grew old enough to ride a leaping horse by himself, waving to parents each time he passed by them. As every Hampton resident knows, that fabled merry-go-round now stands in downtown Hampton, next to the Virginia Air and Space Museum—a revival made possible by citizens' generosity.

The Old Mill Stream was the favorite of courting couples. It was a canal ride in a large wooden bateau, propelled by a water current in a canal. At the canal's end, the bateau was lifted by an underwater mechanism up an incline so it could come rushing downhill at ride's end, splashing passengers and others waiting for the next trip.

But the leapty-dips were every adolescent's goal. You had to be well into your teens before your parents gave permission for you to ride this frightening monster without parental accompa-

niment. It took extra nerve to ride in the front seat and stare down at the earth, almost vertically, when the roller coaster pitched downhill. There were reports of fainting, injury, or sea-sickness, but the leapty-dips survived.

Why did Buckroe fail?

It had many features similar to the currently popular Busch Gardens and King's Dominion, so the question is a real one. For one thing, the opening of the Hampton Roads Bridge-Tunnel hurt Buckroe by improving access to the larger, more publicized Virginia Beach and then North Carolina's Outer Banks area. The reduction in use of passenger trains also contributed, and Sunday school picnics simply went out of style.

More important, however, Buckroe was the victim of changing tastes and styles. Resorts and amusement areas in America have a short life-span, as each new generation creates its own favorites. Whatever the reason, Buckroe played a lustrous part in many lives before it closed—spun sugar, saltwater taffy, leapty-dips and all.

# 42 Roads Took High Ground

SOME OF THE OLDEST ROADS in North America are on this Peninsula— old dirt wagon trails that began to pierce Tidewater's forests in the early decades after the settlement of Jamestown in 1607. And, some of those early roadways merely followed old Indian trails through the woods.

The oldest Virginia thoroughfare was what Jamestown colonists called the "Great Road to the West." It led across Jamestown's isthmus and thence along to the present State Route 5 and up the Peninsula toward Richmond. Greenspring Plantation was along that road, which was used to cart tobacco for shipment to England.

Because Hampton was Virginia's major port through the seventeenth and the early eighteenth centuries, one of those very early roads ran down the Peninsula from the Jamestown area and Middle Plantation (later named Williamsburg) into Elizabeth City County to Hampton.

Road-building was slow in Virginia's first years, when settlers could travel more easily by rowboat or sailboat over Tidewater's countless creeks and rivers. But horses were soon imported from England—the first in 1611— and "horse paths" and "cart paths" were cut through pine woods. Later, ferries became

Daily Press *Archives*

**Kecoughtan Road was widened to four lanes in the early 1940s**

common means for roadways to ford those creeks and rivers.

Early Virginia governments left road clearing to those who owned the land and needed to travel it to their farms and plantations. Only one wagon road connected the present Hampton and downtown Newport News in colonial times. It ran along what is now called Kecough-

Daily Press *Archives*

**The Boulevard at Indian River in 1933**

tan Road ending at about the present 18th Street in Newport News.

Later, counties began to pay farmers to improve horse paths with sand, marl, and gravel during the winter when farmers were not busy.

In his useful *Tobacco Coast*, Arthur Pierce Middleton lists the many ferries licensed by the General Assembly in colonial times. Ferries were often rowed or sailed, but sometimes they were pulled by ropes across narrow creeks. Before ferries, travelers had to ford or swim across narrow creeks, and wagons had to detour around deep ones.

Virginians are indebted to the French and British engineers who fought at Yorktown in 1781 for our best views of what this Peninsula—eastward toward Hampton and westward toward Williamsburg—looked like during that era, especially the roads.

The Peninsula's face had not changed much when the Civil War struck eighty-one years later; few new roads had been built. There were still only two major westward roads: one from Hampton to Williamsburg and the other from

Newport News to Williamsburg. Union armies moving from Fort Monroe utilized both of the roadways at one time or another and much of the land in between. General George B. McClellan, Union commander, complained about the lack of good maps. The spring rains of 1862 turned the few roads into quagmires and seas of mud. Deep wagon tracks furrowed the land for years afterward.

And then, about 1900, Henry Ford's Model T began to revolutionize America and likewise its roads.

In Hampton, Kecoughtan Road was the first and for awhile the only hard-surfaced twentieth-century link with Newport News. It was a narrow, two-lane affair with a speed limit of thirty miles per hour. Later, the other early cross-routes were Shell Road, Newmarket Road, and Briarfield Road. All were rustic and muddy even in the 1920s.

In World War I, the War Department appropriated funds to hard surface a route from Coastal Artillery defenses at Fort Monroe to permit quick army movement up the Peninsula to Williamsburg, Richmond, and thence westward. The Virginia Department of Transportation says this was one of Virginia's first paved roads, running some 280 miles to the West Virginia border.

Of course, streets within Hampton had been designed several centuries earlier and were paved as the area developed. The same was true for old Chesapeake City, which was renamed Phoebus.

World War II and its aftermath brought the first all-out federal and state programs to link the Peninsula—Hampton and Newport News—with Norfolk, the Eastern Shore and Gloucester. A new Military Highway, now named Mercury Boulevard after the seven Mercury astronauts who initially trained at Langley, linked Langley Field with the James River Bridge. Then, the Hampton Roads Bridge-Tunnel was built, the Interstate Highway System began to girdle Hampton Roads, and traffic began to speed accordingly.

# 43 Crabs and "Crab Town"

HAMPTON WAS CALLED "Crab Town," beginning more than a hundred years ago when crab-picking and shipping plants opened on Hampton River (once called Southampton Creek). Looking at today's city shoreline, it's difficult to envision those waterside crab factories that covered the town in the 1920s and 1930s. Crabbing joined oystering as a major seafood industry in the community and gradually, through the years, supplanted the bivalves as a significant money crop.

The crab-picking houses generally were built on docks along the creeks —Hampton River and nearby waters —and mostly painted red. They all had piers where crabbers could unload their catches and sell them. Inside each pierhouse was the picking room, where mostly African American women bent over piles of cooked, bright orange crabs, separating meat from shell.

A Hampton come-here, James McMenamin from Massachusetts, arrived in the 1870s and started canning and shipping crabmeat. McMenamin and Company was "the largest plant in the world devoted exclusively to crabmeat" until the 1940s when it was bought out by Marion S. Quinn. The site is now occupied by Bluewater Yacht Sales.

The lanky Northerner built his first factory on Hampton River in 1878. A year later, he developed a process to package fresh crabmeat in tin cans that allowed shipment of the seafood throughout the United States without risk of spoilage. According to his granddaughter Ann McMenamin, responding in October 1939 to an article in *Time* magazine, the company's canned crabmeat won medals and certificates at the Berlin International Fisheries Exposition in 1880, the London Fisheries Exhibition in 1883, the Paris World's

Daily Press *Archives*

**Crabs were often sorted at dockside**

Women carefully pick crabmeat at Samuel S. Coston Company in 1907

Fair in 1900, the Jamestown Exposition in Norfolk in 1907, and the Panama Pacific International Exposition in San Francisco in 1915.

Ann McMenamin also shared a letter to the company from Army First Lieutenant A. W. Greely, who established Camp Conger in the Canadian arctic in 1881. He remained there for two years; when relief failed to arrive, he left the arctic and returned south. In 1885, Greely wrote:

> It affords me much pleasure to inform you that of our canned articles none stood in higher favor than the crabs canned by you. I regretted that a larger quantity had not been taken by me. The last cans used, some two years after reaching Conger, were as fresh, palatable and satisfactory as the first.

McMenamin's original plant was destroyed in 1892 and immediately rebuilt on the same site. At the height of the company's business, about sixty crab boats were maintained, and approximately 350 employees, many of them women, were on the payroll. He ran the plant until he died in 1901, after which his sons, James and John, ran the McMenamin plant for the next forty or so years.

Besides the McMenamin crab plant, Hampton had other crab operations including, J. S. Darling & Sons, J. S. Jarvis Packer and Shipper of Crab Meat, L. D. Newcomb Fishing Fleet, and Samuel S. Coston Company. Jarvis, an African American, operated at the foot of Queen Street. Howard Horseman, later Hampton's postmaster, was another crab plant owner. William Evans operated a crab house up Sunset Creek, and the Cartwright crab plant flourished nearby.

Later in the 1920s, L. D. Amory and Co. was established on Hampton River and is the last of the "Crab town" plants. It survives today along with Graham-Rollins Seafood Incorporated in handling and packing a variety of seafood including crabs.

Appropriately called "the black crab king" was John Mallory Phillips. He and other local African Americans who began as watermen owned their own seafood businesses. Phillips had more than a half dozen boats and his family-operated business lasted nearly a hundred years.

Besides attracting lots of buyers to their wharves, the crab plants gave off a heavy stench of boiling crabs. Children often held their noses and said "Whew," when their fathers drove them through Hampton's streets on the way to Buckroe.

Summer was crabbing season in the Chesapeake Bay and its tributaries. As the bay warms in April, millions of hard crabs that buried themselves in the soft mud of the bay and river bottoms in the fall begin to dig out and flood the creeks and rivers again. They grow and reproduce all summer, only to return to their hideaways when winter comes.

Today, although the harvests are the lowest on record, crabs are still among the most valuable marine species in the Chesapeake, bringing watermen millions of dollars wholesale at dockside. The blue crab for decades has been to Virginia what lobsters were to Maine.

Those caught on a line baited with meat might snap at you with claws that can inflict severe pain. In the late 1920s, another harvesting method—the crab pot—was invented by B. F. Lewis of Harryhogan. The crab pot increased the catch and allowed watermen to leave trapped crabs unattended for a day, while they emptied other pots or worked nearby areas.

Most do not consider the blue crab exotic, but many Tidewater citizens would disagree. Until recently, its life span has been unknown to most laymen. Its blue-green shell, which changes subtly with its age and habitat, is a masterpiece of camouflage. A bright contrast is the lipstick red of its claws, especially on the females.

No wonder William Warner called his account of the Chesapeake's favorite shellfish *Beautiful Swimmers*. Warner dramatized the crabs' life cycle to make readers aware of the need for more restraint in catching them, but it didn't help much.

Scores of commercial crabbers work from shoal water to deeper channels, fishing hundreds of crab pots, each marked by a float. Pleasure boaters in the rivers of the bay deplore the crab pots, while water-skiers often zip to and fro between them. Watermen harvest their pots virtually every day, putting new bait in the pots and pouring the crabs into barrels for easier dockside management.

Then there are the recreational crabbers—easily hundreds along the Tidewater shorelines —putting out a few crab pots from their docks, often baited with dead fish. Their catch goes directly into a boiling pot for a fresh day's meal. There is no way the fisheries managers can estimate the numbers caught annually, but it adds up.

The annual crab catch varies, depending on water conditions during the season—and this influences the survival rate of the crab. In recent years, "peeler" crabs have become as much a favorite of devotees as the hard crab. Watermen maintain soft crab floats in which "peelers" are kept until they molt out of their hard shells into a soft one. As the soft shell—mostly made of chitin, the substance found in fingernails—hardens in seventy-two hours, the soft crabs must be taken from saltwater soon after molting and prepared for shipment.

*Hampton History Museum*

**John Mallory Phillips (*top*) and James McMenamin**

# 44 Storms Wreaked Havoc

I N RECENT YEARS, HURRICANES have been increasingly feared because of the coastal cottages and piers they destroy, but Virginia has suffered from such fearful storms ever since Jamestown was settled.

From 1607 until today, more than 170 coastal storms have affected Virginia, including more than fifty hurricanes that have severely damaged the Virginia coastline and its tidal waters. The hurricanes occurred primarily in August, September, or October, months when weather conditions are most likely to breed the tropical weather disturbances that come north from the South Atlantic or Caribbean and strike the Atlantic coast.

Hurricanes produce enormously high winds, which blow ocean waters through the Virginia Capes into the Chesapeake Bay and up its tributaries, and high waves that pound against shorelines. Added damage is created when hurricanes coincide with a period of high tides. Wind-driven waves can easily destroy piers, cottages, and shorelines.

Recent dramatic hurricanes have included Floyd and Isabel, which did more damage inland than along the coast as creeks and streams overflowed their banks sweeping into communities such as Franklin, Virginia. Isabel took its toll as water rose and tides devastated property along the James River. Both caused millions of dollars in damages. One particularly savage storm hit on September 12, 1960, when

*Hampton History Museum*

**Downtown Hampton was entirely flooded in the Hurricane of 1933**

*Peninsula Jewish Historical Society*

The newspaper published only a two-page edition because of the storm

Hurricane Donna blew into Hampton Roads with gusts of wind reaching 138 miles per hour at Chesapeake Lighthouse. It caused three deaths. On September 27, 1985, came Hurricane Gloria, which brought an unusually heavy rainfall of 5.65 inches and did damage estimated at $5.5 million.

One major storm, not listed as a hurricane, but packing a similar wallop, is best known as the Ash Wednesday storm of March 6–8, 1962. The U.S. Geological Survey considers it one of the most destructive storms ever to affect the mid-Atlantic states. It was called a northeaster or nor'easter because of the direction of its winds, which were upward of sixty to eighty miles per hour. An estimated $4 million in damages occurred in Hampton; much in the downtown area was covered by six or more feet of water. Across the mid-Atlantic, thirty-four people were killed and more than $200 million in damages were attributed to the storm.

Probably the most devastating modern storm for Hampton and the surrounding area came on August 23, 1933—a blast that raised the water level in Hampton Roads and the lower Chesapeake Bay nearly ten feet above normal. That storm knocked out Hampton

electric power and killed eighteen people throughout the coastal region.

Water poured into the streets of Hampton, and scores of family cottages, particularly along the nearby beaches of Buckroe and Phoebus, were ruined or drastically damaged. The wind and storm surge combined to cause millions of dollars in damage, especially along the Boulevard shoreline between Hampton and Newport News. So much so that the streetcar line that had followed the shoreline was destroyed and had to be moved inland. The system never fully recovered from the event.

That hurricane, which came before the Weather Service began to give them names, produced the highest water ever officially recorded in Virginia. However, unofficial accounts from September 6, 1667, report a rise of twelve feet in Chesapeake Bay.

Earlier in Virginia coastal history, three great storms—in 1693, 1749, and 1846—were so powerful as to alter coastal features. There were other significant storms like the "dreadful Hurry cane" of 1667, which was fierce enough to destroy an early fortification under construction at Old Point Comfort. Records of weather in Hampton Roads have been kept since the

**High water at the east end of the Hampton Bridge after 1933 Hurricane**

National Weather Bureau established an office in Norfolk in 1871. Previous accounts of storms are found in ships' logs, early newspapers, and letters left by survivors.

One such, on October 29, 1693, was recorded by the Royal Society of London: "There happened a most violent storm in Virginia which stopped the course of ancient channels and made some where there never were any." Similarly, Jamestown's original isthmus was washed away by river turbulence about the time of the American Revolution. It was restored in 1957 by the National Park Service.

Willoughby Spit on the Norfolk shore of Hampton Roads owes its very existence to a hurricane of October 19, 1749. According to one record, "A sand spit of 800 acres was washed up." A hurricane in 1806 added more sand, and Willoughby Spit was formed. During that storm, water reportedly rose four feet and flooded into the streets of the village of Hampton, where trees were torn up by their roots and others simply snapped off.

Historically, maybe the most interesting hurricane came in September of 1775 and has been dubbed the "Hurricane of Independence," the same name as a recent book by Williamsburg author Tony Williams. The storm itself wreaked havoc on the Hampton area. The *Virginia Gazette* reported: "From Hampton we learn that they begin to receive melancholy accounts of the loss of lives in the late storm." High winds and rain accompanying the hurricane smashed the Hampton area, which, in fact, led to a military confrontation between British sailors and colonials.

Many ships were damaged as they were thrown ashore at Norfolk, Hampton, and Yorktown. About twenty-five vessels were run ashore or "irrecoverably gone." One British vessel, the *Otter*, became "hopelessly stranded" in the Back River, near Hampton on September 2. Local citizens, realizing the plight, boarded the tender, captured the crew, secured her goods, and set fire to the vessel, actions that many could call "an outright act of war."

(*Top*) River Street in the Pasture Point neighborhood seemed aptly named after the 1962 storm
(*Above*) Buckroe Beach cottages took a beating during the Ash Wednesday storm of 1962

# 45 Trolleys and Streetcars

THE DELIGHTFUL MUSICAL *Meet Me in St. Louis* fittingly celebrated the era of the trolley car in America—an era that did much to identify Hampton and finally to connect it with Newport News.

The first Hampton streetcars—as they were often called—began service between Hampton and Old Point in 1889. The last trolleys ended their runs in 1946, when they were replaced by buses.

Trolleys were a sort of interim step between the horse-and-wagon and the automobile. Only a few American cities have held onto them—wisely, many believe. (In recent years, some larger cities are returning streetcars to their downtown areas.) But streetcars created unbearable traffic problems on the narrow streets of Hampton and later Newport News. So they had to go.

In the trolley's heyday in the 1930s, one could ride from Old Point to Hilton Village or to Buckroe, and the cost was small. Streetcars met passenger ships at Peninsula docks, and they carried young picnickers to Buckroe Beach and Bay Shore. In fact, those two Chesapeake Bay resorts (one for whites and one for African Americans) were built in the 1890s by the Hampton and Old Point Railway Company expressly as a means of boosting weekend trolley patronage.

Hampton's trolley pioneer was James S. Darling, a Long Islander who came to Hampton after the Civil War and first prospered in shipbuilding and oystering. Then he became president and chief stockholder of the first trolley line from its chartering in 1888 until it merged with two competitors in 1900 to form the widespread Citizens Railway, Light and Power Company. The same company then owned Buckroe Beach.

Darling's trolleys, underwritten by the Schmelz brothers—George and Henry—of Hampton through their private bank, extended their run in 1890 to Newport News in order to carry Peninsula workers to Collis Huntington's new shipbuilding yard. Residential areas sprang up around trolley lines.

In the 1930s, the orange-painted Citizens' Rapid Transit Company (CRTC) trolleys roamed the tracks running throughout the area. Over the motor man's head, a sign warned: "Please do not speak to the motor man. His duties require all of his attention."

The fare was five cents, but you

*Hampton History Museum*

**Streetcar parked at car barn in the 1930s**

**Trolley line stopped near the entrance to Hampton Institute (University) in the 1920s**

could pay a few extra nickels at the various transfer stations in Hampton, Old Point, Buckroe, and Newport News.

Everybody traveled by trolley. Couples would ride those rails in evening clothes to attend a dance at the Chamberlin Hotel or take a briefcase and ride daily to work, often reading the newspaper as they went.

Children waited after school to watch the squeaking trolley car turn the corners and pick up passengers. Although it was illegal and parents warned against it, children put pennies on the track to see them squashed by trolley wheels.

Darling's trolley system was so successful that in 1890 the rival Newport News Street Railway Company was started with Colonel Carter Braxton as head. At first, its cars were horse-drawn, but in 1892 they were electrified and extended to Hampton over the newly built Electric Avenue, now Victoria Boulevard.

When the Hampton and Newport News trolley firms merged in 1896, Frank Darling of Hampton, son of James S., became the first president. Other trolley firms started later, ultimately merging into one local system under John Shanahan.

When the great August 1933 hurricane hit Virginia, it destroyed the trolley tracks along the shore of Hampton Roads on the Boulevard. The line was not rebuilt, but replaced with buses.

Buckroe Beach and Bay Shore continued to attract hordes of summer vacationers until World War II, and many visitors reached them by trolley. Extra-heavy trolley rails were laid at Buckroe so that Chesapeake & Ohio excursion trains from Richmond could deliver their passengers next door to the picnic pavilion.

Freight trolleys as well as passenger trolleys served the area in those early days. Francis Schmelz operated a bakery and confectionery in Hampton and used the morning trolley service to send thousands of pastries each workday to the Newport News Shipyard to be sold by vendors outside the gates at lunchtime.

Trolleys were speedy, too. Some could hit thirty-eight miles per hour on the straightaway

Trolley lines went to the Old Point Comfort wharf in the 1890s

between Hampton and Newport News.

President Shanahan of the Citizens' Rapid Transit Company in 1914 had his own private streetcar with plush carpet, wicker chairs, and brass spittoons. The car could be rented to meet VIPs arriving by boat at Old Point or by train in Newport News.

At the height of trolley operations, sixty streetcars were in use in Hampton and Newport News. At night, they rested at the car barn on Electric Avenue, midway between the two cities.

What eventually happened to the area's abandoned trolley cars? A few of them are still visible today as diners, shops, or chicken coops in suburban sites hereabouts. Others were sold and shipped to South America. Their steel tracks were taken up, largely in World War II, and melted down for wartime use.

When streets are repaired these days and the asphalt taken up, old trolley rails can often be seen within the streets. Those folk who still remember *Meet Me in St. Louis* will also remember "Clang! Clang! Clang! Went the Trolley," sung by Judy Garland. Oh, those were, indeed, the bygone days.

One trolley line operated on tracks parallel to the Boulevard (now Chesapeake Avenue)

# 46 German Sailors in Hampton

AS YOU WALK through the Hampton National Cemetery, past row after row of the white, evenly spaced headstones, it is not difficult is visualize the soldiers, sailors, airmen, and marines who fought—either actively or behind the lines—to preserve America's freedom.

Established in 1862 as one of the first such national cemeteries, the Hampton unit received its first burials, most from the military hospital set up at Fort Monroe after action began during the Civil War Peninsula campaign of 1862. Ultimately, it became a national cemetery in 1866. The nearly five acres of land were officially transferred two years later. Through the years, more land has been added, and the parcel now includes just over twenty-seven acres.

According to records, there are 638 unknown soldiers buried at Hampton, most of them Civil War soldiers who fell during battle. There are also 272 Confederate soldiers buried nearby in a separate section.

Hampton National Cemetery also is the burial site of eight Congressional Medal of Honor recipients—seven from the Civil War and one from the Vietnam War.

But additionally, there are German sailors buried among the other graves. And they bring to mind a much hidden World War II story.

The Germans attempted at least once to send spies ashore: on the Outer Banks of North Carolina in April 1942. A German U-boat carried a crew and intelligence personnel and came near but never on the shore. It's the story of the German boat *U-85*, the first enemy submarine to

be destroyed after Germany had declared war on the United States.

Evidence of the attempted sub landing is provided by twenty-nine gravestones in the Hampton cemetery. Each bears only a German name, without date or other detail.

On April 15, 1942, the day after the aborted rendezvous, the burials were undertaken, but there were no detailed reports of the burials when

Daily Press *Archives*

**Conning tower and gun of typical German U-boat**

they happened. Yes, the navy admitted the bodies were buried at night, but they could say no more. National security was involved.

The story that emerged is an almost-successful German submarine landing on the Carolina coast in the early morning of April 14, 1942. But for the vigilance of an old four-stack destroyer, the USS *Roper*, some of those twenty-nine Germans would have gotten ashore to infiltrate the United States as intelligence agents for the Fatherland.

Unlike the *Roper*, the 500-ton *U-85* was the newest and largest type of submarine the

Germans had launched in their bitter undersea war against Atlantic shipping. Masterminded by the brilliant Admiral Karl Doenitz, Germany had sent out nearly 1,000 submarines to sink American ships and cut off aid to Germany's British and French opponents.

Chesapeake Bay sea-lanes were haunted by

*United States Navy*

**The USS *Roper* chased *U-85* through the night**

Doenitz's wolf packs, as the submarine groups were called. Offshore sinkings were often visible from the Outer Banks, which Carolinians called "Torpedo Alley." Debris from sunken ships and from vanished crewmen often floated ashore onto the quiet beaches that extend from Virginia Beach south to Cape Hatteras.

Lacking new destroyers, the navy had pulled World War I four-stackers out of mothballs and set them to work combating Doenitz's undersea fleet. That's how the USS *Roper* happened to be steaming south from Hampton Roads on the night of April 13, patrolling the coast southward from Cape Henry to Cape Hatteras.

At midnight, a new watch took over. The spring night was clear and starlit. The sea was almost calm, and glints of phosphorus brightened the ship's wake. To starboard, men on duty could see Wimble Shoal Light off North Carolina's Outer Banks.

Then, at six minutes past midnight, the *Roper*'s radar showed an object bearing 190 degrees true at a distance of 2,700 yards. Lieutenant Commander Hamilton Howe, the captain, decided to investigate. The *Roper*'s underwater

detectors soon picked up propeller sounds, which confirmed the radar.

Howe increased speed to twenty knots and lookouts began to spot the wake of a small vessel running away at high speed. As the *Roper* closed on her prey, Howe sounded battle stations and ordered all weapons ready to fire. As the *Roper* gained ground, the invisible object changed course radically. The *Roper* changed too, pulling up to within 700 yards of the unknown adversary.

Suddenly a torpedo sped toward the *Roper*, narrowly missing. The destroyer had *U-85*, on its second Atlantic voyage, on the run.

"When the distance had been reduced to 300 yards, the fleeing vessel cut sharply to starboard," Howe reported to his Navy superiors.

At this instant, using the 24-inch searchlight, she was identified as a large submarine moving on the surface. The searchlight was held on her and first machine guns opened fire, then three-inch battery. The machine guns cut down the submarine personnel rushing to man their guns.

At that moment, young Coxswain Harry Heyman, manning Gun 5, scored a direct hit on the U-boat's conning tower. It was his first shot in combat. The *Roper*'s crew saw water begin to pour into the ruptured submarine.

In the glare of the *Roper*'s searchlight, the German crew scrambled wildly out of the disabled sub as she began to sink. Screaming and shouting, they plunged into the waters, some without life jackets.

Howe ordered a torpedo fired to finish the submarine, but *U-85* sank before it could be discharged, settling stern-first into the Atlantic about sixteen miles southeast of Nags Head. Because German subs hunted in wolf packs of two or three, Howe ordered his ship to circle cautiously and drop depth charges. He had heard of skippers torpedoed by a second sub while attempting to

**Secret night burial, a day after sinking**

rescue submarine crewmen, and he wanted to protect against it.

With the Germans still writhing and shouting in the water, the *Roper* dropped a barrage of eleven depth charges. The powerful underwater concussions killed those Germans not already dead. Some of the Germans were dressed in civilian clothes and were preparing to embark in a rubber raft when the submarine was attacked. When recovered, their wallets were found to contain American currency and fake identification cards.

The *Roper* had averted a night landing of German espionage operatives along the lonely Carolina coast, not far away.

For the rest of the night the *Roper* scoured the area for other subs. Her radioed reports to the navy at Norfolk—kept brief to avert enemy detection and pursuit—brought a navy PBY patrol plane at daybreak to look for oil slicks and debris. Two more planes joined and began dropping smoke floats to lead the destroyer to German bodies kept afloat by life jackets. Before the two-hour operation had ended, seven planes, a navy dirigible, and a British trawler were helping.

Clothing and dog tags gave the names of the twenty-nine dead Germans hauled aboard the *Roper*. Two were officers, one the *U-85*'s skipper. From empty life jackets floating in the water, it could be seen that others had sunk beneath the waves.

The sunken sub site was marked with a buoy, and the *Roper* then returned to port.

The bodies were transferred to the Norfolk Naval Air Station for intelligence evaluation. They were buried in Hampton later that night. Protestant and Roman Catholic chaplains read the burial service by lamplight, and a squad of navy seamen fired the volleys in salute. Passersby were mystified by the nocturnal rites. One of them called a newspaper reporter in Newport News, and that was the first hint at the larger story.

So it is today that those young German sailors lie beneath the magnolias of Hampton, while *U-85* rests in fourteen fathoms off the Outer Banks in the graveyard of the Atlantic.

**Recent service recognizes German sailors**

# 47 Military Bases at War

WAR ALWAYS BRINGS attention to military bases, and, in Hampton Roads, activities at bases such as Hampton's Langley Field demonstrate the importance to the region of the military components in our communities.

In the pre–World War II years on the Peninsula, Uncle Sam was building up the army, navy, and the army air corps at Langley. Once the war got fully under way, military bases and civilian industries, like Newport News Shipbuilding and Dry Dock Co., worked round the clock.

Langley Field was especially exciting in those days because of the emerging potential of

*Library of Congress*

**A-20 Havoc bomber at Langley Field in 1942**

aviation in warfare. Air corps officers like Hap Arnold, Carl Spaatz, Bob Stratemeyer, Ira Eaker, Frank Andrews, and Arnold Krogstad were showing what airplanes could do. All would become famous in the war.

There was a mission flown from Langley Field to South America by a force of Flying Fortresses led by Colonel Robert Old. It was billed as a "good-will mission" to Brazil, Argentina, and Colombia, but actually it was to impress the world with America's airpower.

"Flyboys" at Langley Field were thought by local girls in those days to have more than their share of pizzazz. Beirne Lay, who married a Hampton girl named Ludwell Lee, was an example. Besides flying, he wrote *I Wanted Wings*, which became a hit movie. And Langley's Flying Fortresses and their crews took part in MGM's successful *Test Pilot* in 1938, with Spencer Tracy, Myrna Loy, and Clark Gable. Some scenes were filmed at Langley.

A lot was going on, too, at NACA—the National Advisory Committee on Aeronautics—also quartered at Langley Field. (It was the predecessor of NASA.) Daring young men were testing new aircraft. Peninsula boys resented them because they dated local girls—from Hampton and its surroundings. Most of them had zippy roadsters and wore beards, to which Peninsula high schoolers were unaccustomed.

One of the "NACA nuts," as they called themselves, was Eastman Jacobs, an interesting scientist who retired to the West Coast; he died in 1987. Jacobs was responsible for advancing many fields of aerodynamics, dealing particularly with airfoils, turbulence, boundary layers, and Schlieren photography. He headed the wind tunnel research for more than a decade. Other NACA pioneers, such as Richard T. Whitcomb and Robert R. Gilruth, lived nearby.

A great boom in housing went on in Hampton and elsewhere in the region to accommodate the buildup of military personnel and shipyard workers. Businesses grew to serve both military requirements and the increased population base.

Nearby Fort Eustis in Warwick County was initially established in 1918 as a replacement for Fort Monroe's coastal artillery school. It was revived in 1940 and used again for coastal artillery. In 1946, it became home to the army's new transportation center and school.

When America entered the war after Japan's December 7, 1941, attack on Pearl Harbor, most of the young men—in their late teens, twenties, and early thirties—went off to fight. Many of the military officers who had been stationed at Peninsula bases became famous.

Chief among these was Dwight Eisenhower, who had served at Fort Monroe as a lieutenant colonel. Other Fort Monroe alumni who were given high commands in the war were General Courtney Hodges and General Joseph T. McNarney.

From Langley Field, Colonel Walter Weaver, who had predicted Hitler's blitzkrieg in 1938–1939, became a three-star general, commanding the Army Air Technical Training Command, which prepared soldiers to repair and service airplanes.

At the shipyard, old hands remembered a slim young officer named Raymond Ames Spruance, who had served his first post-Annapolis duty as a naval shipbuilder in Newport News. He became one of the great admirals.

*United States Army*

**Early entrance to Fort Eustis**

Much of what went on on the Peninsula during World War II was shrouded in secrecy. The navy kept secret all data on warships under construction or repair. And the Hampton Roads Port of Embarkation did its best to send its transports loaded with GIs out into the Atlantic Ocean without letting anybody know. That's because German U-boats lurked beneath the sea-lanes, waiting to torpedo any vessel leaving or entering the Capes.

A submarine net was strung across the main Hampton Roads channel from Fort Monroe to Willoughby to enmesh any enemy U-boat trying to enter. And U.S. Navy convoys left port under cover of night to reduce the danger of enemy detection.

World War II has been over for decades, and the cold war that followed ended with the fall of the Soviet Union in the early 1990s. Then came two desert storms in wars with Iraq. Changes have come within the U.S. military establishment, and bases are being consolidated and reorganized. Historic Fort Monroe will soon be retired as an active installation with many of its responsibilities, departments, and personnel transferred to Fort Eustis.

# 48 Spratley Decision Sets Precedent

THE PENINSULA HAS produced a lot of good judges, but the most celebrated one in the twentieth century was Claude Vernon Spratley Jr. of Hampton, who rose through judicial ranks to be a justice of the Virginia Supreme Court from 1936 until he retired in 1967.

Two important cases at Hampton in the 1930s spread his reputation and led Governor George Peery to appoint him in 1936 to Virginia's high court. The first case was the trial of Dr. Elisha Kent Kane III in 1931 on the charge of drowning his wife.

The other was his decision in 1933 that an African American man could not be barred by color from voting in a primary election. Such flagrant racism was often taken matter-of-factly

then. Judge Spratley, however, had no hesitation about his decision, though he knew it would be opposed by many Virginians. As he saw it, "I couldn't see any more reason for a man to be denied this right because of brown skin than because of brown hair."

A lot of Hampton and Newport News citizens revered the jaunty judge. He lived to be 94, dying in October 1976 after having retired at 85 from Virginia's high court.

He kept his wits and lively humor to the end. At his funeral, St. John's Church was packed with statesmen, judges, and Hamptonians. The service was conducted by Bishop John Bentley, the retired bishop of Alaska, and the Rev. Francis Hayes.

The voting rights case was brought by L. E. Wilson, a well-regarded African American man who worked for a Hampton building and loan association after election judges had refused to let him vote in a primary on August 1, 1933. They were simply following the usual Southern practice. They argued in their defense that "party plans of the Democratic party limited the right to vote in the primary to white persons only."

Wilson then brought suit against Democratic officials. He said he had met all conditions of residence and poll tax

Daily Press *Archives*

**Judge C. Vernon Spratley Jr. at the Hampton Courthouse**

payment. He was represented by attorneys J. Thomas Newsome of Newport News and A. W. E. Bassette Jr. of Hampton. When the case was heard by Judge Spratley in circuit court, the judge concluded that Wilson had been entitled to vote. As he put it:

> I held that the primary was being held in accordance with statutory provisions; that the expenses thereof were paid from the public funds: that the statute itself prescribed the qualifications for a right to participate therein and did not exclude a person by reason of his color; that although the primary plan of the Democratic party provided only for participation in its primaries by white persons, the provision was in conflict with the law and the law prevailed; and that, therefore, a Negro could not he denied the right to participate in such primary merely because of his color.

As expected, Judge Spratley's decision provoked wrath. "It was thought by some political sages at that time that his career as a judge was finished," said his friend Thomas B. Gay of the Richmond firm of Hunton, Anderson, and Gay. But others felt the judge was right. *The New York Times* ran the story on its front page, headlining it "Negro Vote Ruling Surprises Virginia."

Most Virginia newspapers applauded the decision. Attorney Ben Jacobs of Newport News wrote to one paper that Judge Spratley's "just and courageous ruling" had been handed down in a Virginia court, without pressure or agitation. He felt the decision "pointed the way to proper adjustment of race matters" and had "not left any bitter after effect."

Although Hampton Democrats asked party authorities in Virginia to appeal the decision, they failed to do so. When the issue of African American voting came to trial in other Virginia localities, all the other judges followed Spratley's lead.

In his thirty-one years on the state Supreme Court, Judge Spratley wrote an opinion for the majority in 664 cases and for the minority in 74 others. In his entire judicial career, he made or took part in 7,000 opinions. Governor Lindsay Almond, himself a lawyer, praised

their "crystal clarity" and "marked erudition."

Although he remained an independent spirit, Judge Spratley was a strict constructionist. He felt the Supreme Court had no power to reshape laws passed by Congress or the Virginia General Assembly. In one dissent, he wrote:

> We have nothing to do with the wisdom, policy, or expediency impelling the makers of the Constitution in drafting the fundamental law. Whether the law, as written, be harsh or unjust, contrary to "ancient usage," or contrary to expediency, as we view it, we cannot correct same, or relieve against it.

Judge Spratley's humor endeared him to many people. In his office he usually wore a green plastic visor, like an old-fashioned pool

Daily Press *Archives*

**Judge Spratley loved gardening**

player. Like many men of his era, he liked to chomp on a cigar while he worked. Often he wore in his lapel a sprig of azalea or a rose from his yard on Hampton's Columbia Avenue, cut from the garden planted by his wife, the former Annie Woodward of Hampton, who died in 1948.

The judge was born in Surry in 1882 of an old county family. He graduated from William and Mary in 1901, aged 19, and taught math and Latin in Hampton and Newport News schools to save money to enter the University of Virginia Law School. He said he made his first dollar folding crabmeat price lists for James McMenamin, a Hampton crab-packing operator. He began his law practice in Hampton in 1906 and became Hampton's city attorney in 1912. He held that office until appointed judge of the circuit that included Hampton, Elizabeth City, and Newport News. A good friend was Judge T. J. Barham of Newport News Corporation Court, who had also been born in Surry.

Judge Spratley and his contemporaries were an interesting lot, including such colorful courtroom pleaders as J. Winston Read, Allan D. Jones, Thomas Newsome, Charles C. Berkeley, A. L. "Allie" Bivins, Charles E. Ford, Lee Ford, Sclater Montague, and Fay Collier. Of more sedate style were R. M. Lett, Philip Murray, W. B. and Shep Colonna, Fred Skinner, John Marshall, Herbert G. Smith, Sinclair Phillips, Billy Carleton, Frank Blechman, and some others.

Attorney E. Ralph James, who, like Judge Spratley, came to Hampton from Surry, remembered how Judge Spratley welcomed him his first day in court: "All good things have their beginning either in Surry or at William and Mary," the judge said. "You came from both, so you're doubly blessed. You'll get along all right."

Judge Spratley always maintained his boyish enthusiasm, even in his 90s. He loved parties and repartee. A fellow Hamptonian once listed the judge's hobbies as "golf, canes, gardens, loud-barking dogs, weekend visits, buttonhole bouquets, social intercourse and entertainment, and snappy ensembles in dress." Old photos will vouch for the snappy ensembles.

And Judge Spratley adored circuses. Said an old friend, "He would have adjourned the Kane murder case to go to the circus." That was Judge Spratley.

Daily Press *Archives*

**A younger Judge Spratley addresses law conference**

# 49 Ferry Boat Connections

WHEN THE HAMPTON ROADS Bridge-Tunnel opened in 1957, it replaced two ferry lines that formerly operated between the Peninsula and Norfolk.

One was the Old Point Ferry, which crossed Hampton Roads on a route that closely follows today's bridge-tunnel. The older and more frequent service was offered by the Newport News Ferry, which ran between the Boat Harbor and Pine Beach, now part of Norfolk Naval Base.

The Old Point Ferry, connecting Hampton with Willoughby Spit, was started in 1925 by F. J. McGuire and J. M. Hayden, who incorporated the Hampton Roads Transportation Co. Their Old Point dock was at Fort Monroe, close to the Chamberlin Hotel, while their Willoughby Spit dock was at the point where the Hampton Roads Bridge-Tunnel now reaches the Ocean View mainland.

The Newport News–Norfolk Ferry initially was created by the Commonwealth of Virginia in 1907 for the Jamestown Exposition. It allowed easier ways for potential exposition visitors to reach the fairgrounds from the west. Ultimately, the Norfolk Street Railway Co. took over the service from the state.

In 1912, the Chesapeake Ferry Co., organized by Fergus Reid, well-known Norfolk financier and cotton exporter, bought Norfolk Street Railway. In its first years this ferry ran between Manteo Avenue in Newport News's east end and Pine Beach.

The Newport News site was later moved to the Small Boat Harbor. (The old dock for the

Daily Press *Archives*

**The automobile ferry was vital before the tunnels were built**

Boat Harbor ferry became the construction headquarters for the Virginia Department of Transportation for building the Monitor-Merrimac Memorial Bridge, a 4.6 mile connection that opened in 1992.)

The availability of cross-channel ferry service was one reason why the navy established the Norfolk Naval Base in 1918 and why the army set up Langley Field and Fort Eustis the same year.

Trolleys connected with the ferry at each dock of both railway operations. The first ferryboats were passenger steamers, unequipped for vehicles. Then, as autos came into use, vehicular ferries were introduced in 1912. After years as competitors, the two ferry operations merged in 1929 under the Chesapeake Ferry Co.

Daily Press *Archives*

**The Hampton-to-Norfolk ferry connected both sides of Hampton Roads**

Both lines bought most of their boats from northern ferry lines, one vessel retaining the name *Ocean City* until it ended service. Others bore names like *Warwick, Willoughby, Sewell's Point, Hampton Roads, Chesapeake, Hampton, Norfolk, Old Point Comfort* and *Newport News*.

For a while in the 1950s, the ferries were run by the Virginia Department of Highways, now the Department of Transportation. When the Hampton Roads Bridge-Tunnel opened, the ferry boats were sold to out-of-state buyers or transferred to the state's Jamestown-Surry service farther west on the James River.

Both early ferry lines used large steel vessels with capacity for many autos and foot passengers. The ferries had refreshment stands, and some of them had a second deck upstairs where passengers could sit out the twenty- to thirty-minute ride, watching ships in the harbor.

The ferry lines, prompt and dependable, were heavily used during the two world wars. In the 1940s, the schedule of daily trips on each line was doubled. Just before departure, each ferry boat blew a farewell blast, bringing cars rushing down the pier to get aboard before the gate was closed.

Many romances between ferry passengers developed over the years, according to some commuters. The ferry was also a good place for servicemen to pick up rides, and they often solicited drivers to give them a lift. The ferries occasionally suspended service during hurricanes and other severe turbulence. However, they set good records for safety and reliability.

The first Hampton Roads ferryboats were sidewheelers, but gradually stern-wheel propellers were preferred. Harold S. Sniffen, former curator of the Mariners' Museum, wrote in 1946, "of the nine vessels still in service on the Newport News–Pine Beach run, four are sidewheel steamers, but only one or two are still used."

The hulls of the vessels were black, with "Chesapeake Ferry Company" painted in white. Windows at the level of automobile doors enabled patrons to view the crossing.

Atop the vessel were pilothouses. Between them, a tall black smokestack stood and lifeboats were stored. The ferries' demise, which corresponded to quicker means of passage over Hampton Roads, nevertheless, represented the end to an era of quiet, slow transit.

# 50 Buckroe Beach Memories

A GAUDY CHAPTER of Peninsula history ended in the 1960s when the once-prosperous Buckroe Beach resort in Hampton was shorn of many of its "delights" and converted by federal grants into a prosaic Hampton coastal suburb.

One of the many who mourned its change was Warren McNamara Sr., who devoted his life to Buckroe until he retired in 1980 and moved to Florida.

McNamara discovered Buckroe as a boy in 1938 when he came by Baltimore steamer to Old Point. "The next day I rode the streetcar from the Langley Hotel to Buckroe," he said. "I was so excited with it that when I was offered an amusement ride job at $10 a week, I went to work." In the next forty-two years, he created a Buckroe hardware store, motel, hotel, bath-house, summer cottages, and a dozen amusement attractions.

In later years, he built McNamara's Pier 1 Restaurant, which flourished on the Buckroe shore until set afire in 1971 by an arsonist. Rebuilt, it operated nearly a decade longer.

The lively entrepreneur was always full of enthusiasm for Buckroe.

> At 76 years, I feel young again at [a] request for information. My mind is excited by the memories. But there does remain some bitterness at the unforgivable failure of Hampton to recognize just what Buckroe Beach was and could [have been].

McNamara's most dramatic memory is of the rumored night visit of a German submarine to the Buckroe shore near the Salt Ponds in January 1942, during World War II. "It was

*Hampton History Museum*

**Fabled carousel, built in 1920, shown here in 1931**

reported that a German sub had put ashore a boat or raft," he said. "One rumor claimed that the raft or boat contained three uniformed Germans. Immediately, the U.S. Military erected five lookout towers on the beach." The towers were manned by Civil Defense volunteers.

In McNamara's early Buckroe years, people would rent a waterfront bathhouse cubicle for twenty-five cents to change clothes for swimming. Men were at first required to wear tank tops.

Chesapeake & Ohio Railway excursions in Buckroe's boom years were daily occurrences, the big steam engines puffing over Pembroke Avenue to disgorge at the Buckroe waterfront. McNamara recalled:

> Excursion trains included a "lockup" car, and the C&O provided police service in case a passenger drank too much beer or started a fight. … Sometimes there were so many train coaches they had to return from Buckroe to Phoebus until needed. Those same rail tracks were also used by the Newport News-to-Buckroe streetcar.

In those days, the governor often came to Buckroe for a Labor Day speech and fireworks. The three-story Buckroe Hotel, which stood across Resort Boulevard from the beach, was known for its shore dinners featuring Buckroe spot. Amusement park employees could buy a bargain Sunday dinner for twenty-five cents. When World War II began, the government leased the hotel; it was demolished after the war.

McNamara remembers such early Buckroe enterprises as the Sans Souci Motel, Todd's cottages, Gordon's cottages, A. T. Hull's Log

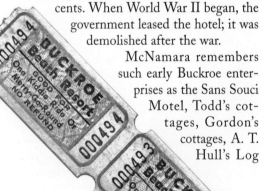

**Amusement park tickets**

Cabin Hotel, Novell's cottages, and Groves' Hotel. Many houses had "Room to Rent" signs. Says McNamara, "Owners took pride in cleanliness, maintenance and landscaping."

A familiar sight was "William the Crab Man" with his waterfront pushcart. "William's wife made the best deviled crabs in Virginia," McNamara proclaimed, "and the public knew it. He would set out early, for Richmond people would buy them by the bags full to carry home."

The amusement park was developed at the beginning of the twentieth century by the Peninsula Street Railway System, owned by Hampton's James S. Darling. Later, Virginia Electric and Power Co. became owner until federal laws in 1954 compelled VEPCO to divest itself of Buckroe. Then, the park was bought by Peter Stieffen, who also had a cigar store in Newport News. Buckroe was then at its height, with hordes of soldiers and sailors from nearby bases and many of the 27,000 men and women at the shipyard visiting often, sometimes daily.

The yard paid its blue-collar workers in silver dollars, McNamara recalled, and they often fell out of their owners' pockets. "As shipyard people rode the roller coaster and other rides, they would often leave their seats with silver dollars dislodged by the roller coaster's motion," he remembers. "Ride employees who were paid only $5 to $7 weekly might find as much as $20 in silver dollars left behind on busy nights."

McNamara mischievously admits to making good profits selling bottles of Chesapeake seawater.

> We bought bottles and half filled them with water. The label read, "This is ocean water. Do not fill but half full because when the tide rises it will break the bottle, if filled."

Bottles cost McNamara two cents each and sold for fifteen cents. Thousands were bought.

McNamara fondly remembers the Buckroe pavilion, where Eddie Travis led the Jolly Jazz Orchestra for nightly dancing. Tickets were ten cents a dance or three dances for a quarter.

A third of a mile away on the Chesapeake Bay was Bayshore, an amusement center for African Americans. A group of Hampton Institute (now University) people owned it, and such

**Amusement park in the '50s**

stars as Ella Fitzgerald, Pearl Bailey, Duke Ellington, and Cab Calloway played there.

McNamara cherished his memories: "The laughter of children, the romance of older people listening to Eddie Travis sing 'People Will Say We're in Love.'" Now it's all gone, but not quite.

A big part of Buckroe Beach memories is alive and well, but removed to downtown Hampton. The merry-go-round that entertained so many people for more than a half-century was acquired by the City of Hampton in 1986 when the amusement park finally gave up. The forty-eight horses and two chariots that carried so many of us on glorious gallops was back in business.

The carousel began life in 1920. Built by the Philadelphia Toboggan Co. (No. 50), it is one of only 200 or so classic survivors of the 3,000 merry-go-rounds that once turned across America.

Hampton's June McPartland, who has done research on carousels, said the first one was built for French nobles in the sixteenth century.

**Buckroe's broad, sandy beach always attracted a crowd**

Originally, the ride was for adults, who tried to spear metal rings as the carousel whirled. About 1870, a steam-driven carousel was invented in England, permitting a much larger circle.

Carousels came to the United States in the 1860s when German immigrant Gustav Dentzel began making them as a sideline of his cabinet works. The Buckroe Beach carousel—one of the finest—was built by German, Italian, and Russian artisans working in the Philadelphia shop.

The restored and rebuilt carousel reopened in 1992 in a pavilion adjacent to the Virginia Air and Space Museum.

# 51 Andrews—A Senate Power

HE WAS ACERBIC, FORMIDABLE, temperamental, hard to deal with, and manipulative, but Hunter Booker Andrews was also brilliant, honest, sincere, and a politician of great guile, whose word was his bond—an unusual quality these days for politicians.

But Andrews was not of these days. His time was from 1964 until 1996 when he was an eight-term state senator. His family came to the colony of Virginia in its very early years, and Andrews, without a doubt, understood and appreciated his own history as well as the history of his beloved Commonwealth of Virginia.

If Judge C. Vernon Spratley Jr. was Hampton's most outstanding jurist of the twentieth century—and that probably goes without question—then Hunter Andrews was its most outstanding twentieth-century politician. Period.

*The Washington Post*, reflecting on the career of Hunter (it was often pronounced "Huntah") Andrews, stated: "he wielded enormous clout during the three decades when the Democrats controlled every branch of the state's government and his power often matched that of the nine governors under whom he served."

Andrews was proud

Daily Press *Archives*
**Hunter B. Andrews**

of his heritage—of the fact that branches of his family, the Whitings and Beverleys, came to Virginia before 1620. A later ancestor, Colonel Thomas Whiting, was an important Virginia landholder and member of the colonial House of Burgesses. He served as godfather for the infant George Washington, holding the baby in his arms at baptism. In the days before the Revolution, Whiting was also the king's attorney and, during that war, served as president of the naval board.

Andrews's family also is traced from the colonial Wythe family through Anne Wythe, the sister of the famed eighteenth-century legal mind George Wythe of Hampton, who sired no children. Wythe, signer of the Declaration of Independence, was the first law professor at the College of William and Mary, where Andrews gained his undergraduate degree in 1942.

Andrews's grandfather Hunter Russell Booker was an important Hampton businessman in the early twentieth century, having started Merchants National Bank in 1903. He also operated a local hardware store. It was Booker who brought to the attention of his fellow towns- and countrymen his wish that a history of Hampton be compiled as a matter of civic concern. This was done in 1922 by Lyon G.

Tyler, retired president of William and Mary. The Bookers' homeplace was Sherwood, later to become part of the sprawling Langley Air Force Base.

After attending William and Mary, Andrews served in the navy in the Pacific theater during World War II and returned to earn a law degree from the University of Virginia in 1948. He immediately began to practice law in his native Hampton, where he was considered a very good, but expensive lawyer.

His first public service was as a member of the Hampton School Board from 1958 to 1963. As school board chairman in 1961, it took only a handshake with Vincent J. Thomas, chairman of the Norfolk School Board, to formally establish WHRO-TV, which began to operate channel 15, Virginia's first noncommercial educational television station.

In November 1963, Andrews ran for his first elected post in the Senate of Virginia and was reelected to seven subsequent terms, a political legacy matched by few state politicians in the twentieth century. Slowly, but with determination, he began to show his ability to get bills adopted and to solve legislative dilemmas. By 1979, he pulled a coup and gained the majority leader position, and, in 1986, he became the powerful chairman of the senate finance committee upon the death of longtime senate leader Edward Wiley of Richmond.

Former Governor Mills E. Godwin Jr. said Andrews knew more about the state's budget operation than anyone else, including the budget writers.

Holding the two most powerful senate posts simultaneously, Andrews was the leader. *The Washington Post* observed:

Daily Press *Archives*

**Andrews with House Speaker Tom Moss in 1992**

His reputation was that of an aristocratic and irascible leader whose mastery of the state budget and encyclopedic knowledge of the law could reduce a freshman legislator to tears, even without being subjected to his withering glare. His whim could derail a bill, and a barbed remark could deflate a bloated ego, former colleagues recalled to the Associated Press.

One of his senate colleagues said of him,

He was a born leader who did not suffer fools gladly. He had guts and courage and talent and great compassion for the less fortunate. We all felt his wrath, but we all felt his passion too.

There are countless Hunter Andrews stories. During floor debates, he would regale his audience—supporters and opponents alike—with words of Oliver Cromwell, Shakespeare, and Washington and other Virginians. A fervent Anglophile, he reportedly had the rug in the senate chamber replaced with a carpet of burgundy, copying the color in the British House of Lords. He also supported obtaining a coat of arms for the senate from the College of Arms in London.

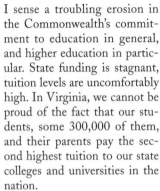

Daily Press *Archives*

**In formal attire**

He served for many years as a board member of the Jamestown-Yorktown Foundation, the state agency that operates Jamestown Settlement and the Yorktown Victory Center, and was its vice chairman and chairman for a decade or more.

A *Richmond Times-Dispatch* reporter wrote:

> A story, possibly apocryphal, goes that teenage pages in the State Capitol some years ago were told to give visitors a tour of the Senate. They made one stop, and one stop only: the office of Senate Majority Leader Andrews.

Through the years, Andrews engineered the passage of budget bills with millions of dollars designated for education — higher education, secondary education, almost any education. He felt support of Virginia's colleges, universities, and schools was of paramount importance. In a commencement address at the University of Virginia, he summed up his feelings:

> I sense a troubling erosion in the Commonwealth's commitment to education in general, and higher education in particular. State funding is stagnant, tuition levels are uncomfortably high. In Virginia, we cannot be proud of the fact that our students, some 300,000 of them, and their parents pay the second highest tuition to our state colleges and universities in the nation.

Hunter's beloved wife, Cynthia Bentley Collins, was his solid supporter. The daughter of a member of the Virginia House of Delegates, she understood the world of politics.

Hunter Andrews died in January 2005. When he was defeated for reelection in 1985 another of his senate colleagues observed, "Guys like Hunter only come along once in a generation. He may be the best legislator in the whole country."

Daily Press *Archives*

**Andrews with wife, Cynthia**

# 52 Fort Monroe: an Overview

FORT MONROE, the nation's oldest military fortress in continual use, will cease active operations in 2011. Its future has not yet been determined, but its historic legacy has long been assured.

It is called, "The Gibraltar of the Chesapeake" or the "Defender of the Chesapeake." Those titles say it all.

The point, known as Point Comfort from the early Jamestown days in Virginia and for more than two centuries as Old Point Comfort, sticks out into the edge of the bay: a sentinel keeping guard.

The focus of the point is Fort Monroe, a large, moated stone fortress, over which the flag of the United States has flown throughout the base's nearly 200-year history. That fact itself is amazing since it was located amid the Confederate States of America for four years but was never yielded by Union forces.

Like many military installations, Fort Monroe was created because of a war—the War of 1812. During that conflict, the British sailed unimpeded up the Chesapeake Bay from Hampton Roads to the Potomac River and on to Washington, D.C., the capital of the young nation. British troops stormed the city in August 1814 and burned many public buildings, including the White House, the president's mansion.

After the war, military tacticians vowed never to permit another coastal assault and directed the establishment of a series of coastal fortifications along the Atlantic and Gulf coasts. One of them would be Fort Monroe, named

after President James Monroe, a Virginian and the country's commander in chief when construction was begun in 1819.

Brevet Brigadier General Simon Bernard reportedly designed the fort. He came to the United States in 1816 after being banished from public life in France, where he had served for

Harper's Weekly, *February 2, 1861, Editor's Collection*
**Sea battery and lighthouse at Fort Monroe**

many years in the army and risen to the rank of brigadier general. President James Madison appointed him "assistant engineer." Bernard ultimately headed the engineer board that supervised the new coastal fortifications.

Captain William T. Poussin, Army Engineers, drew the plans from Bernard's design— "a regular work, with seven fronts [with bastions], covering about sixty-three acres of ground and surrounded by an eight-foot deep moat," varying in width from 60 to 150 feet. It was designed to accommodate 380 guns, but that number was never achieved. Construction was finally completed in 1834 at a cost of nearly $1.9 million.

When finally completed, it was the largest fortress of its kind in the United States. A companion outpost, Fort Calhoun, was built on a shoal off Old Point Comfort (*see* Chapter 12) as an additional guardian for Hampton Roads. It was later renamed Fort Wool.

The fort's history, a remarkable succession of events that parallel the 19th- and 20th-century history of the United States Army, was captured in a definitive account, *Defender of the Chesapeake: The Story of Fort Monroe*, written by Colonel Robert Arthur in 1930. In 1978, Richard P. Weinert Jr., command historian at Fort Monroe, revised, edited, and updated the volume. A subsequent third edition was published in 1988 also under Weinert. The book is heavily footnoted and contains an eight-page bibliography, a list of commanding officers, a list of higher headquarters, and a list of all the troop units stationed at the fort through 1987.

A number of pictorial histories of Fort

*Casemate Museum Collection*
**Simon Bernard**

Monroe, including the most recent, *Fort Monroe* by Paul S. Morando and David J. Johnson, add to the visual documentation of the fortress.

Fort Monroe's history is dotted with the names of significant military leaders: Robert E. Lee was at Monroe in the early 1830s supervising construction; Joseph Johnson and Jubal Early, later Confederate generals, also worked at the fort while they were U.S. Army personnel.

The first military units at Fort Monroe were artillery outfits intended to man the great guns installed to guard Hampton Roads, the entrance to the Chesapeake Bay. The Army's Artillery School of Practice was created there in 1824 to train thousands of young soldiers.

Early in its history, U.S. presidents Andrew Jackson and John Tyler visited Monroe (*see* Chapter 12) and the adjacent Fort Calhoun. Other visiting presidents included Abraham Lincoln (*see* Chapter 15), Rutherford B. Hayes, and James A. Garfield (*see* Chapter 22).

*Casemate Museum Collection*
**Hygeia Hotel and Fort Monroe as Civil War began, circa 1861**

In the 30 years prior to the Civil War, the fortress carried out many responsibilities, including serving as "host" to Indian Chief Black Hawk and several of his subchieftains, who were captured at the end of the "Chief Black Hawk War." They were sent to the post until President Jackson decided they could return home. Subsequently, during the Seminole Indian outbreak and for about five years when the army was focused on the Florida area, Fort Monroe served as a base for troop assignments.

According to Arthur's history of the fort, a resort-style atmosphere began to develop at Old Point Comfort on land just south and outside the fort during these years. The Hygeia Hotel was built and began to attract the society and wealth of the South in the way that Saratoga in New York attracted similar clientele of the era.

During the Mexican War, the fort was again the center for recruits. Another presidential visit occurred on June 21, 1851, when Millard Fillmore arrived on the steamer *Baltimore* for a brief visit. In 1858, the army established a second artillery school at Monroe.

The Civil War brought an entirely new focus for the fort. Suddenly, in April 1861, the army found itself on the edge of a new nation: the Confederate States of America. All the surrounding land—for a few weeks at least—was enemy territory or, at best, was beset by Confederate patrols from nearby Yorktown, a Confederate base.

The first skirmish between Confederate and Union troops after Fort Sumter's bombardment occurred only weeks later on June 10, 1861, at Big Bethel Church, just a few miles away. Those Union troops came from Monroe. About that time, the fort began its role as a "safe haven" for runaway slaves and, after the Emancipation Proclamation of January 1, 1863, for emancipated African Americans who were seeking security.

In 1862, General George McClellan embarked upon his infamous Peninsula Campaign, which, if he had handled it right, could have resulted in major triumphs. Instead, it merely produced a continuing list of Union disappointments and misdirections.

A recently found letter, written by Sergeant Charles Brown of Company H, 16th Massachusetts Infantry, from Waltham, Massachusetts, offers some interesting observations regarding the artillery at the fort. In a letter

*Casemate Museum Collection*

**Robert E. Lee, a Fort Monroe lieutenant**

home, dated April 20, 1862, from Camp Hamilton, a Union Army encampment just outside Monroe, Brown wrote:

> Went to the fort yesterday. Saw some big shot for union's gun. They are long cylinders square both ends about two feet long and one foot in diameter. They think these may strike a fairer blow than the conical slugs, not as likely to glance. Irwin and Lincoln [names given the two guns] are mounted side by side and command the channel.

A month earlier, the famed battle between the *Monitor* and *Merrimack* (renamed the *Virginia*) was fought in Hampton Roads, across the water near Sewell's Point. The duel between the two ironclad vessels on March 9 ultimately ended in a draw.

Sergeant Brown continued in his letter: "The gunner Welch says he can hit the *Merrimac* [*sic*] 20 times before she can get out of range. Hope the *Merrimac* will come out and

**Nineteenth-century Fort Monroe is encircled by twentieth-century military post**

fight." After repairs, the *Merrimack* did return to the water, but neither Brown nor other Union troops saw the ships fight again. Brown died of wounds he suffered at Gettysburg, Pennsylvania, on July 4, 1863.

During part of the war, General John E. Wool was commander of Fort Monroe; subsequently, Fort Calhoun was renamed Fort Wool in his honor.

With the end of the Civil War and the collapse of the Confederacy, its president Jefferson Davis was captured in Georgia on May 10, 1865. About twelve days later, he was brought to Fort Monroe, along with former Confederate Senator Clement C. Clay, to await trial on charges of treason. The new commander of Fort Monroe, Major General Nelson A. Miles, treated his new prisoner with disdain. Davis was placed in an open casemate—No. 2—and Clay in No. 4, while casemates Nos. 1, 3, and 5 were occupied by guards of soldiers. Davis and Clay

were never to be left alone, Miles ordered.

A lamp was kept constantly burning in each of the prisoners' rooms. The furniture for each was a hospital bed with an iron bedstead, a stool, table, and a movable stool closet. A Bible was allowed each, and afterward a prayer book and tobacco were added.

Although not receiving any direct orders to do so, Miles ordered that Davis be placed in irons two days after his arrival. Miles reported to C. A. Dana, assistant secretary of war, that "irons [were] put on Davis' ankles, which he violently resisted, but became more quiet afterward. His hands are unencumbered." Five days later, after a communication from Secretary of War Edwin M. Stanton, the shackles were removed.

Davis persistently complained about the unheated, open casemate and its lack of healthful air. Lieutenant Colonel Dr. John Craven, the post's chief medical officer, agreed and complained to commanders about Davis's plight. Finally, on October 2, 1865, after more than four months of imprisonment, the ex-Confederate president was transferred to a larger room

*Casemate Museum Collection*

**Jefferson Davis imprisoned in casemate**

in nearby Carroll Hall, where he remained until May 1867, when he was released on a habeas corpus writ.

In May 1866, Varina Davis came to Monroe to visit her husband and began to live in a casemate apartment. In December, Davis's accommodations at Carroll Hall were expanded, and his wife was allowed to move in with him during his last six months at the fort.

After the war, the artillery school was resumed, but life at the fort, and throughout the Army moved very slowly. The urgency of combat was gone, except for those soldiers in the West who were involved in the Indian Wars.

By the late 1880s, Fort Monroe and the army were reawakening. The post was overhauled, and its coastal defenses upgraded with larger and more modern guns. The area surrounding the post was also revived with a new Hygeia becoming a "resort" under the ownership of Harrison Phoebus.

The outbreak of the Spanish American War ended the artillery school because most of the soldiers were drawn away into more active service areas farther south. After that conflict, the school was resumed and the fort again modernized. In 1907, the artillery elements were separated, and Monroe became the center for the coast artillery training, while field artillery was moved elsewhere.

During World War I, the coast artillery program was increased, and training camps established at the fort. Initially 1,200 officer candidates came for training; later another

*Casemate Museum Collection*

**Fort Monroe with moat, and the Hygeia and Chamberlin hotels (*background*), about 1900**

was moved elsewhere.

During World War I, the coastal artillery program was increased, and training camps established at the fort. Initially 1,200 officer candidates came for training; later another 1,277 attended, while a third camp enrolled 613. Camp Eustis, on Mulberry Island along the James River in Warwick County, was created to handle crowded conditions at Fort Monroe and to train enlisted men. Named for General Abraham Eustis, the first commander of Fort Monroe, the training camp ultimately became a part of the artillery school.

Like the rest of the army, the time between the wars was a military lull. Armaments at Monroe were gradually improved during this time with installation of a wide-ranging group of coastal artillery weapons. Additionally, the army maintained submarine barriers and underwater mine fields. By World War II, the fort was in the forefront of coastal defense systems. However, by the end of the war, all the coastal armaments became obsolete with the enhancement of aircraft carriers and long-range bombers.

Since the late 1940s, Fort Monroe has been the headquarters for the training of soldiers. First, it was headquarters of the Continental Army Command, established in 1955 to handle all training and operational control of army ground forces. In a 1973 reorganization, the command was divided. One element became the United States Army Training and Doctrine Command, headquartered at Monroe, while the United States Army Forces Command was assigned elsewhere. This responsibility for training soldiers for war has remained the mission of TRADOC and its host facility Fort Monroe.

In 2005, the Defense Base Closure and Realignment (BRAC) Commission placed Fort Monroe on a list of bases to be closed or realigned. Monroe is scheduled to be closed sometime in 2011. Commissions are currently at work determining how the closure will be carried out and what will be the future of the fortress and related property. One requirement of the closure will be the protection of all historic property, especially the rock-walled fort.

William Shakespeare in *The Tempest* probably said it best and in relation to Fort Monroe: "The past is prologue."

*—Wilford Kale*

*Casemate Museum Collection*

**Entrance to Casemate Museum in Bastion 1**

# EXPANDED ILLUSTRATION CREDITS

# INDEX

*Hampton History Museum*

**The Richelieu, a Phoebus saloon, circa 1900**

Harper's Weekly Magazine, *September 20, 1862, Editor's Collection*

**The Army of the Potomac passes in review in front of the Old Hygeia Hotel in 1862**

*Author's Collection, Virginia State Library*

**Bathing beauties at Buckroe Beach Hotel in the 1920s**

© Janus Images

**Guarding Fort Monroe in 1864 is the "Lincoln Gun," a fifteen-inch Rodman**

*Editor's Collection*

**Hygeia Dining Saloon and Port Office on the "Baltimore" Wharf at Old Point Comfort, 1864**

Tignor, W. T., Store, 74-75
*Times-Herald*, 51, 85-87
Tribune, Co., 87
Trolley Lines, 48-49, 88, 119, 124, 126-128, 147
Truman, Harry S., President, 46
Tuskegee Institute, 56
Twain, Mark, 72, 84
Tyler, John, President, 31-33, 46, 156
Tyler, Julia Gardiner, 32
Tyler, Lyon G., 16, 23-24, 152

*U-85*, 139-141
USS *Virginia*, 92
USS *Roper*, 139-141

Van Buren, William R., 87
Van Buren, William R., Jr., 52, 86-87
Vardon, Harry, 78
Virgin Islands, 13
Virginia (colony & commonwealth), 1, 4, 5, 6, 7, 8, 9, 11, 19, 23, 32-34
*Virginia* (pinnace), 1, 2
Virginia Company (See London Company)
*Virginia*, C.S.S. (See Merrimac)
*Virginia Gazette*, 7, 16
Virginia Institute of Marine Science, 122
Virginia Marine Resources Commission, 122-123
Virginia Supreme Court, 144
Virginia, University of, 28
von Zeppelin, Ferdinand, Count, 113

Walker, Emma Dean, 56
War of 1812, 17, 18, 25-27, 32, 47, 69
War Memorial Stadium, 80
Warner, William, 131
Warren, Sir Boarlase, Admiral, 27
Washington, D.C., 25, 27, 39, 64-65, 69, 82, 84, 100, 110, 119, 155

Washington, Booker T., 56-57, 81, 83
Washington, George, 5, 22
Weaver, Walter, Colonel, 101
Weinert, Richard, Jr., 38, 156
West, George Ben, 69
West Point, New York, 28-29
West, William, 41
Whittier, John Greenleaf, 54
Wilson, Harvey L., 87
Wilson, James Southall, 28
Wilson, L. E., 144-145
Wilson, Woodrow, President, 79-80, 105
William and Mary, College of, 6, 10, 16, 19, 21-22, 122, 146, 152-153
Williamsburg, 11, 14, 23-25, 32, 36, 43, 48, 89-90, 128
Wolfe, Fred, 109
Wolfe, Thomas, 102, 107-109
Wool, John Ellis, Major General, 33, 39, 45, 158
World War I, 33, 76, 90, 97, 99, 101, 105, 110. 113, 124, 128, 159
World War II, 33, 76, 98, 103, 115, 119-120, 125, 137, 142-143, 149, 153
Wright Brothers, 105-106
Wright, Orville, 106
Wriothesley, Henry, 3
Wyatt, Francis, Governor, 4, 5
Wythe, Elizabeth Taliaferro, 22
Wythe, George, 21-23, 102, 152
Wythe, Margaret Walker, 21
Wythe, Thomas, 21
Wythe, Thomas I, 21

Yorktown, 34, 36, 58
Young, William P., 26

# THE AUTHOR

Parke Rouse Jr., a native of Smithfield, Virginia, was a journalist, administrator, and gifted writer of numerous history books about Tidewater Virginia—its people, places, and things.

A graduate of Washington and Lee University in 1937, he began his newspaper career at the Newport News *Times-Herald* and, just prior to World War II, with the *Richmond Times-Dispatch*. Rouse served as a naval officer in assaults in the Mediterranean Sea and later in the Pacific. After the war, he returned to the *Times-Dispatch* until 1950 when he joined the Virginia State Chamber of Commerce. Three years later, he became director of publications for Colonial Williamsburg. He resided in Williamsburg for the next forty-plus years.

In 1954, the Commonwealth of Virginia named him to direct the 350th anniversary festival commemorating the English landing and settlement of Jamestown in 1607. He remained with the Jamestown-Yorktown Foundation, a state agency, until his retirement in 1980. During those years, he also served as director of the state's bicentennial commemoration in 1976.

Rouse returned to his roots in newspapers and began writing a weekly Sunday column for the Newport News *Daily Press*. His topics were varied but stressed local Tidewater history and recalled events and people of his youth and the lifestyles of those bygone days.

Through his career Rouse wrote more than twenty books including the well-known *Below the James Lies Dixie, The Great Wagon Road: From Philadelphia to the South*, and *The James: Where a Nation Began*.

In 1988, Governor Gerald Baliles proclaimed Rouse a Virginia Laureate for his contributions in preserving the Commonwealth's heritage. Two of his anecdotal histories, *Cows on the Campus: Williamsburg in the Bygone Days* (1973) and *We Happy WASPs: Virginia in the Days of Jim Crow and Harry Byrd* (1997) about Richmond, have become treasures.

Rouse died in 1997, but in 2006 another of his books was published: *Jamestown's Story: Act One of the American Dream*. Compiled and edited by Wilford Kale, another Williamsburg journalist, the book contains stories and articles written by Rouse about the seventeenth-century Jamestown settlement.

*Thomas L. Williams*

**Parke Rouse, Jr.**

# THE EDITOR

Wilford Kale, a native of Charlotte, North Carolina, and a resident of Williamsburg, Virginia, for nearly fifty years, has written extensively about Tidewater Virginia as a newspaperman and author.

A College of William and Mary alumnus, he graduated from Park University in 1971, after serving as an army officer during the Vietnam War. He is currently a master's degree candidate in history at the University of Leicester, Leicester, England.

Mr. Kale began his newspaper career in 1960 at the Charlotte *Observer*, working as a high school student in the sports department and later during the summers and holidays of his college years. In 1966, he joined the Williamsburg News Bureau of the Richmond *Times-Dispatch*.

Following military service, Mr. Kale returned to Williamsburg as bureau chief of the *Times-Dispatch*, serving until May 1992, when he became a senior writer on the paper's Business News staff in Richmond. He left the paper in December 1993 and immediately joined the management team of the Virginia Marine Resources Commission, a state agency in Newport News, Virginia, where he served until 2006 as senior staff adviser.

His first book, *Hark Upon the Gale, an Illustrated History of the College of William and Mary*, was published in 1985. It was the first encompassing history of the college in eighty years and the first-ever illustrated history. It was republished in a redesigned and expanded form in 2007. Mr. Kale has written numerous articles for magazines and edited *Johnny Walker, His Dreams, His Success and His Vision*, and coauthored *Davis Y. Paschall: A Story in Leadership*.

In 1998, he was the lead writer of *Goal to Goal: 100 Seasons of Football at William and Mary*.

In 2006, Mr. Kale compiled and edited a group of stories by Parke Rouse Jr. Entitled *Jamestown's Story: Act One of the American Dream*, the book describes the early years of the English settlement of Jamestown, Virginia, in 1607.

Kale has been the recipient of numerous writing and journalism-related awards and honors. Most recently, in the spring of 2009, the Virginia Professional Chapter, Society of Professional Journalists presented him with its Distinguished Service Award, an honor given on only nine occasions in the past 30 years.

*Walker W. Kale*

**Wilford Kale**